Praise for *Shields of Strength*

"Kenny Vaughan's journey from fear into faith should encourage anyone who has ever dared to dream big. His down-to-earth struggle is one everyone will relate to, and his triumph over adversity will make you want more of what he has—the security of knowing that God is in control!"

Chuck Holton
Military correspondent for CBN
Author of *A More Elite Soldier* and *Bulletproof*

"Kenny Vaughan's book allows us to confront our personal demons of fear and trust by providing the hope that is found in God's word. His wise counsel comes from his own struggles, and his "Shields of Strength" have given hope to so many service members. As the Pentagon Chaplain after 9/11, I saw military and civilians alike find hope in God's word through a simple 'dog tag' and its reminder of God's severity. Kenny has walked the walk, and now, his words and shields allow others to realize that God is really in control of everything. The concept works not only for athletes and soldiers, but for all of us who struggle. I pray that his book will give you the hope and strength that I have found in it and the shield that is with me always, reminding me of a way less traveled."

Colonel Ralph Benson
Pentagon Chaplain

"As representative for Fort Hood, Texas, the largest military installation in the free world, I am very happy to endorse Kenny Vaughan's new book, *Shields of Strength*. I have seen first-hand the tremendous impact of his Shields of Strength, the 'dog tags,' in the lives of soldiers, their families, and those who love and support them. My wife, Erika, and I both are reminded of the sacrifices of those who serve when we wear our own 'dog tags.' God bless Kenny and his work with our military."

Rep. John R. Carter,
Member of Congress, Texas District 31

"Kenny Vaughan is the best public speaker I have ever observed in my twenty-two years of military service. He inspires, motivates, encourages, and challenges everyone to overcome fear by trusting in God. His message is simple, powerful, biblical, and timely. His personal struggle and victory over years of fear and failure solidifies his credibility and fuels his humility. He continues to touch the lives of countless American soldiers and their families as they faithfully fight the war on terrorism and endure years of separation, fear, and hardship. When I read Joshua 1:9, I think of Kenny Vaughan."

Colonel David Dodd
United States Army

# of Shields Strength®

One Man's Victory Over
Fear and What It Has Meant
for America

Kenny Vaughan

Brown Books Publishing Group
Dallas, Texas

Shields of Strength

One Man's Victory Over Fear and What It Has Meant for America

© 2010 Kenny Vaughan

Brown Books Publishing Group
16200 North Dallas Parkway, Suite 170
Dallas, Texas 75248
www.brownbooks.com
972-381-0009

A New Era in Publishing™

ISBN-13: 978-1-934812-74-7
ISBN-10: 1-934812-74-9

LCCN: 2010929440
1 2 3 4 5 6 7 8 9 10

This story is for every athlete, soldier, and student; every spouse, parent, and single parent; every businessman and woman; every son and daughter— every soul who desperately needs to see that God is much bigger and more powerful than his or her own struggles, fears, and emotions.

Special thanks to my beautiful wife, Tammie, for your faithful love and for teaching me how to have the heart of a champion.

TABLE OF CONTENTS

FOREWORD

I first encountered the Kenny Vaughan story when I was working on a book about faith and America's soldiers. My research led me to the tale of Captain Russell Rippetoe, the first American killed in Iraq to be buried in Arlington National Cemetery. Because of this honor, Captain Rippetoe was mentioned by President Bush in his 2003 Memorial Day speech, and the clothing and equipment Captain Rippetoe was wearing when he died were put on display at the Smithsonian Museum. This is how I first learned of Kenny.

Among Rippetoe's effects in that display was a dog tag–like piece of metal with a modified version of Joshua 1:9 printed on it: "I will be strong and courageous. I will not be terrified, or discouraged; for the Lord my God is with me wherever I go." I was intrigued when I first saw it, and after researching further, I came to understand that these were called Shields of Strength, that they arose from the championship water ski jumping career of Kenny Vaughan, and that thousands in the armed services carried them, including, for a while, the commander in chief.

It moved me that Kenny had first developed the Shields of Strength out of his own battle with fear. He had intended them to help other athletes with their own inner battles, but in time the troops in Afghanistan and Iraq began finding them inspiring, and before long millions could be found in American military installations around the world.

I began to understand how much Kenny's story and the shields meant to our troops when I was embedded with U.S. forces in Iraq in 2005. I saw Marines read them aloud and kiss them before roaring their humvees down the famously dangerous Route Irish. I watched chaplains give them to "newbies," and I marveled at how a wounded airman gripped his Shield of Strength while a nurse dug shrapnel out of his leg. I also saw them hanging around the upended rifles of the dead. From six thousand miles away, Kenny Vaughan was ministering to our warriors with little pieces of metal and with the story you'll find in this book.

I did not know Kenny personally when I included his work in my book, *The Faith of the American Soldier.* I still did not know him when I told of his victory over fear in *American Heroes: Stories of Faith, Courage, and Sacrifice from the Front Lines.* Once he read what I had written about him, though, there was no way Kenny and I were not going to meet. You see, Kenny Vaughan is as graciously Cajun as any man you can know, and as soon as we first spoke by phone, the invitations never stopped. I had to head to Beaumont, Texas. There had to be a feed. Did I like to fish? Was I a hunter? We would do it all, Kenny promised, and I should get ready to eat more than I ever had in my life. Just get yourself down here, I was told.

What I found when I finally made my way to southeast Texas is that Kenny is as passionate about life as he is about God and the truth of His Word. We talked and we laughed and we spent hours in his airboat catching gators. Yes, gators. There are pictures. And we ate like there was no tomorrow. We also assured each other that Kenny's brother, Gabe—a fine and honorable soul—is also the king of Planet Crazy, and yes, there would have to be bigger food fests to come.

All fun aside, my time with Kenny and his family taught me what God can do with a man who is willing to trust Him, who is willing to confront his fears, and who offers what he has learned to those who need it most. In short, I was changed by my time in Kenny Vaughan's presence.

I trust that you will be just as changed by what you read here. Kenny will be the first to tell you that he is no superhero, but he has allowed his life to be a conduit of God's grace, and millions have been affected as a result. I believe that you can be as well. Then I hope you will not only live the truths you learn here but also help Kenny continue to touch lives around the world.

We live in desperate times, and only a people of desperate faith can master them. Kenny Vaughan is about to show you how.

—Stephen Mansfield
New York Times bestselling author

PROLOGUE

Everything in my life is defined as either before or after that moment in 1996. I was competing in the USA Water Ski National Championship competition in Fort Walton Beach, Florida. I was skimming across the water. My speed behind the boat was approaching sixty miles per hour. The jump I was about to make would take me nearly three stories into the air for a distance of about three quarters of the length of a football field.

For seventeen years, I had been working toward this day. These were years of rigorous physical training and discipline. I had learned to push myself and perfect my skills. As I approached the ramp that day in 1996, I could not have been more prepared physically. I was about to learn, though, that physical training is not enough. I learned that one cannot win a spiritual battle with only physical training. I learned, too, that faith in God is not something you can halfway, almost, or sometimes have. He will bring you to a day when you either have faith in Him or you don't. He will challenge you out of cautious faith to absolute faith. That's what He did to me.

Now, in the championship competition for which I had prepared most of my life, sixty of the country's best skiers were striving for the title. The skier before me had jumped five feet farther than my personal best. My mind was waterlogged with worry, and the boat pulling me seemed weighed down with my doubt. On my second of three jumps, I had hung my right ski on the side of the ramp, snapping off the fin and tearing the ski boot that held my foot to the ski. Between my second and last jump, I had time to change the fin but no time to fix the boot. The judges called time for me, and I knew I must ski then or forfeit. There was really no way for me to win with a torn ski boot, but there simply was no time to repair it.

Soon I felt the boat accelerate, and I was up. The water was smooth, but the choppy waves of my emotions swirled around me, threatening to throw me off balance. My inner turmoil swelled, fed by years of almost winning, years of getting close but never quite making the mark of a champion, of living the trial but never going home with the trophy. I had moments of believing in the power of God, but I never fully trusted, never fully tested the promises of God, so I always ended up holding onto the ski rope more tightly than I held on to God. Nearly always, my fear propelled me toward failure at a greater speed than any boat could have pulled me.

Heading now for the ramp, the wake of emotion broke with enough force to suck me under. I knew I was nearing the ramp with a speed too slow and a position too narrow on the boat. I could feel a part of me watching from the dock, then turning slowly and slinking away in defeat. All I could possibly do was lose—again. Then I caught a glimpse of the words my girlfriend had painted on the handle of my tow rope, a passage from Philippians 4:13: "I can do all things through Christ who strengthens me." I decided that this time I wouldn't let my fear finish for me. I would finish to the glory of God and let Him take me all the way to victory or defeat. This time I would live out my faith to my last ounce of strength and concentration.

In retrospect, I see how God brought me to that moment of crisis. Every day since, He shows me more about why He took me through the trials the way He did. Every day, I find more meaning in my wild ride up the ramp, holding so tightly to His hand. I am ahead of my story, though. I should go back and start at the beginning.

ACKNOWLEDGMENTS

I want to thank my parents, Robert and Alice Vaughan, for the countless hours they spent pulling us on our skis nearly every day of the summer, for all the personal sacrifices they made because they always put us first, for the love and discipline we constantly received, for teaching us good work ethics, and for pouring all the wisdom they could into us.

I want to thank my wife, Tammie, for leading me to the Lord. Tammie supported me and believed in me when I needed it most. Her love and stability are the foundation to my testimony, and next to the Lord, she is my greatest source of strength.

I want to thank Tammie's parents, Frank and Eloise Roccaforte, for taking me as their own and for raising Tammie to love the Lord and others with such a sincere heart.

I want to thank my sister, Bonnie, and my brother, Gabe, for picking me up the many times I fell and for challenging me to be a better person and athlete. The three of us have always been very close, and we are one another's greatest fans.

I want to thank my pastor and uncle, Richard Vaughan, and David Hinson for being my spiritual mentors.

I want to thank my ski coach and boat driver, Charlie Fontenot, for believing in me when I did not believe in myself and for the years he's spent teaching and encouraging me to be a champion.

I want to thank Command Sergeant Major Jacqui Clay, Chaplain Larry Toney, Mr. and Mrs. Jim Blanchard, and Chaplain Gregory Schannep for taking the first Shields of Strength to the military.

I want to thank Colonel David Dodd; his wife, Sharon; and their daughters, Caitlin and Grace; for their service to our country, for sharing the shields with so many members of the military, and for the Dodd family's wonderful friendship.

I want to thank Russell Rippetoe for giving his life in defense of our country and his parents, Lieutenant Colonel Joe Rippetoe and Mrs. Rippetoe, for their continued support of Shields of Strength. The Rippetoe family has paid the ultimate price, yet they remain the ultimate patriots.

I would like to thank Mark Alexander and *The Federalist* readers for helping to fund over fifty thousand Shields of Strength for U.S. Marines, sailors, and soldiers in Iraq.

I want to thank Marcia Davis-Seale for taking a letter I wrote to a soldier, pouring her heart into it and helping me transform it into *Shields of Strength*.

I want to thank Stephen Mansfield, Beverly Darnell, and Chartwell Literary Group for all you have done to encourage me and for helping me to update this book. Thank you, Stephen, for the generous forward and the hours you spent helping me pull it together.

I would also like to thank Mike Rhodes and Rhodes Design, not only for designing this cover, but for fourteen years of design and artwork. Thanks so much Mike for all your hard work and dedication to our mission.

"Call to me, and I will answer you,
and show you great and mighty things,
which you do not know."
—*Jeremiah 33:3*

"Many are the plans in a man's heart,
but it is the Lord's purpose that prevails."
—*Proverbs 19:21*

The Kingdom of heaven is like a mustard seed planted in a field. It is the smallest of all seeds, but it becomes the largest of all trees.

Matthew 13:31-32

Shield of Strength

CHAPTER ONE

HUMBLE BEGINNINGS

I grew up around the water, fishing and boating. I suppose it was only natural that I would learn to ski eventually. I remember that I was ten when my Uncle Wade invited my family to his lake house for the Fourth of July weekend. That's when my parents decided to teach us—my brother and sister and me—to ski.

My first ski equipment may have been crude, but the rough rope and broken broomstick we used as a ski tow handle must have tied a line around my heart and bound me with a love for the sport that has never grown slack. That boat, a fourteen-foot flat bottom with a fifteen-horsepower Evinrude motor, pulled us on a sheet of plywood my dad had cut into a three-foot circle. The plywood was easy to "ski" on, and my sister, brother, and I could all ride on it at the same time. My mother and father spent hours pulling us behind the boat, up and down the river on that makeshift plywood disk.

Sometime later, I remember that I was fishing when I heard the hum of an approaching boat and looked up to see my sister skiing down the river as my father piloted the boat. She was on skis this time—not a piece of plywood—and the sight of it was nearly too much for me. I dropped my rod and ran to the water's edge, waving frantically and yelling at my dad to bring the boat back for me so I could try. I admit that I was drawn by the adventure, but I also did not want to let my younger sister accomplish something that I couldn't. So I was motivated as I launched into this second skiing experience. Taking my sister's place, I quickly found my "ski legs" and was soon gliding down the river behind that Evinrude outboard. I could never imagine all that was to follow this little sibling rivalry and my small taste of victory.

Today I ski on the most advanced skis in the world and behind the world's most powerful competition ski boats. I wear as many as twelve pieces of equipment for safety and performance enhancement, and any one of those pieces costs more than my father paid for all of the equipment I used while learning to ski. My first ski equipment was makeshift and crude but crafted out of love by my father. Beginnings do not have to be fancy to be meaningful. I have learned not to discount the humble and the simple beginnings in life. God can take little and make much—and aren't we glad!

The Bible is filled with such accounts. In Matthew 13:31, Jesus says, "The kingdom of heaven is like a mustard seed, which a man took and planted in his field. Though it is the smallest of all seeds, when it grows, it is the largest of garden plants and becomes a tree, so that the birds of the air come and perch in its branches." In Matthew, chapter 25, Jesus tells a story of three men who were given talents, each according to his ability. The more the man's ability, the more talents the master gave him. Two of the men took the several talents they were given and multiplied them. To these men, their master said, "Well done, my good and faithful servants. You have been faithful with a few things; I will put you in charge of many things." The third servant took the only talent he had been given and buried it. He had the least to lose and the biggest fear of all the men. To him, the master said, "You wicked, lazy servant." The master took the talent from him, gave it to the one who worked the hardest to multiply his talents, and said, "For everyone who has will be given more, and he will have an abundance. Whoever does not have, even what he has will be taken away from him." What I have learned and what I believe God is trying to say with both of these stories is that He wants us to take what we have and do the best we can with it, trusting in Him implicitly. When we learn how to multiply little things with God's help, then He will be able to teach us to multiply bigger things. That leads back to humble beginnings. The number or degree of gifts or talents we have does not make the difference. Trusting God to help us apply and multiply them makes all the difference.

For me, an unforgettable example from the Bible is when God told Moses to go before Pharaoh. Moses asked, "Who am I, that I should go before Pharaoh and bring the Israelites out of Egypt?" Moses had nothing but a cane and a huge confidence problem. Still, Moses took what little he had and put it to work for God. You know the rest of the story—God used that cane to part the Red Sea. He later gave Moses the Ten Commandments and the responsibility of leading the Israelites out of the wilderness and helping them find the Promised Land. Moses knew he wasn't capable of completing all these tasks on his own. But Moses finished big because he followed God's lead. He didn't give up, no matter how impossible things seemed, and he trusted God to make the way. Take what you have been given, no matter how simple or insignificant it might seem to you, and use it for the Lord!

CHAPTER TWO

THE COMPETITION

In the years following those first experiences on skis, the sport quickly became more of a passion for me than a pastime. After that first summer, I found myself skiing as much as I fished. I found out that I was pretty good, and I began working to hone my skill. I skied in my first tournament at the age of eleven. I wanted to get even better and so I trained—hard! After one training session I found myself going home with a friend whose name was Charlie Fontenot. Charlie loved skiing, too, and as we talked that day, he began telling me about the nationals and how he had won a championship medal. My heart leapt within me as a dream was born in my soul—the dream of winning a national competition medal. Little did I know to what heights and depths that dream would carry me. My path seemed clear, but I could not know how much more God had planned for me. I thought I understood the prize, but God had set His sights on so much more for me. By the way, I also could not have known that my companion that day—Charlie Fontenot—would become my driver and ski coach of many years.

Dreams require sacrifice and hard work, and I paid my dues. Within a couple of years, I was skiing well enough to qualify for the state and regional ski tournaments. I was learning fast and moving up in the sport more quickly than most of my age-level competitors. At the age of thirteen, though, I faced my first big setback when all of my competitors hit a growth spurt while I seemed to have stopped growing. For the next three years, my success was hindered by the fact that I hardly grew an inch. I soon found that I was much smaller than the boys I was competing against. Once a month my parents drove me to Galveston, Texas, where specialists monitored my growth to determine if I would need growth hormones. The situation was painful for me. While I was striving my hardest to become a champion athlete, doctors were trying to determine if my body had simply stopped developing. My parents and I began to realize that

I might never be "normal." By the time I was a sophomore in high school, I was but half the size of my competition. I felt I was living out the epic of David and Goliath on the waterfront and the ski circuit. Standing four feet eleven inches tall and weighing 100 pounds, I was dwarfed by the other high school skiers. In fact, I gained only an inch during my entire sophomore year.

During my junior year, I skied well enough to qualify in the regional tournament as a favorite to place in the top three. That placement would qualify me for the national tournament, a benchmark in my dream quest. That was in 1983, and it would have been great if God had planned for me to win that year—but it wasn't to be. He had a longer, more arduous course set up for me, a course that would bring me closer to Him and would allow my ski trials to take on more meaning than I could ever imagine.

Before I go much further in my story, I'd like to tell you a bit of what it is like to jump on water skis. I want to take some time with this because if you understand my sport, you'll understand better why the fear that dominated my life brought me such horrible defeat. Besides, I think you'll find ski jumping exciting! The boat I ski behind is called a Ski Nautique and is built specifically for pulling tournament skiers. Ski boats are not built for high speeds but instead for lots of power. Their top speed is only around fifty miles per hour, but they could just about pull your car off the bank with their power. Because the top athletes pull so hard on the boat, nothing else is able to maintain the boat speed when the skier is cutting his way to the ramp. I remember skiing behind a friend's bass boat one time, and when I cut from one side of the boat to the other, I looked to the boat and saw that his eyes were as big around as dinner plates. Then I realized I had turned his boat completely sideways and it was just about to flip over. When we got back to the bank, we realized I had also pulled the eye (where the rope was tied) on the back of his boat right out of the fiberglass.

Ski boats don't need to be very fast because the maximum speed that the American Water Ski Association rules allow a ski jumper to be pulled is thirty-five miles per hour. This is much faster than you may realize. This maximum of thirty-five miles per hour is what creates an even playing field for all jumpers. From there it is up to the jumper to build extra speed for a long jump, and he or she does this by skiing up on one side of the boat, turning sharply back toward the other side, and then quickly crossing behind the boat and up beside it on the opposite side. When this maneuver is done correctly, a jumper will reach nearly seventy miles per hour after crossing behind the boat and then passing it again on the opposite side. As you can imagine, water when you are going sixty plus miles per hour is very hard, almost like concrete. If you fall at sixty plus miles per hour, you won't go into the water; you will bounce—and even worse. I always tell people if you want to know what it's like to crash on jump skis, have a friend drive you at sixty miles per hour over a two to three story bridge with water under it and jump over the guard rail as you pass over. Now, you have to do this only after you have tied a seven-foot board on each foot. As you can imagine, it's bad enough to crash into the water, but when you throw in those two boards, it can get really bad really fast.

Because of the potential for injury, skiers wear all kinds of gear for protection. We also strap our right arms at the elbow to our sides because the force of the pull when we cut is too strong for any jumper to keep his arms from being pulled straight out from the shoulders, which results in too high a center of gravity and makes the jump even more dangerous. So having our right arms tied at the elbow to our waists helps ensure a lower center of gravity plus a safer and longer jump. In addition to that arm sling, we wear a helmet, a mouthpiece, gloves, knee braces, a back brace, and a rubber padded wet suit. I also wear an arm guard (that prevents my ski from breaking my arm on a landing) and a foot brace to protect an old Lisfranc fracture. The last thing I put on to cover all this gear is called a speed suit. It is designed to help with wind resistance and to eliminate all the drag that occurs at high speeds on all that equipment we wear.

When I start pulling my gear out, I begin to focus on what I need to accomplish and what conditions I have—such as the wind or where the sun is. Usually, the first piece of equipment I put on is my knee brace. When I start putting on that first knee brace, my mind starts gearing up. From that point until I am finished, I have no interest in talking. I do my best not to be short with people, but I just can't focus on anything else. My heartbeat starts picking up and I get more and more focused as I pull on all my gear. By the time I am ready to ski, I am not sure I could hold a conversation with someone if I had to.

After I have all my gear and skis on, I am normally sitting on the end of the dock with my skis hanging over the edge above the water. Instead of getting in the water, I prefer to leave from the dock. If I can keep from getting wet, I feel like my speed suit is more effective. Also, water-soaked gear moves around on my body more than dry gear, and I like everything to stay put. Most of the time I won't even get wet. I will leave from the dock, take my jumps, then ski back up to the dock and get back up on it just before I sink—often nearly completely dry—unless it is a really hot day. On those days all the gear warms me up so much that it feels good just to jump in the water.

Once the boat pulls away and I am up skiing, I immediately make a few hard short cuts just to get my muscles ready for all the strain they will be under. As I pass the ramp heading to the other end of the lake, I like to look at the surface as long as possible. I just stare at it trying to get that picture in my mind and remind my brain of what is to come. A ski jump happens so fast that most of your actions are really more like reflexes or immediate decisions based on what you see than conscious decisions.

The ride down the lake is nice and slow and is an opportunity to evaluate all the conditions and feel the water. Believe it or not, some water is fast and other water is slow. Everything on the way down the lake getting ready to set up for your return toward the ramp is peaceful and comfortable up until the boat begins the 180 degree turn to head back to the ramp. About mid-turn I hear the boat's engine start roaring. It is a deep rumble because the tail pipes are right on top of the water coming out of the rear of the boat. Then immediately I feel the power come down the rope and everything changes. I know that as we enter the turn it's time to get into a strong position. The peaceful part is over. I want to be in a strong position when the power comes from the boat because otherwise it will pull me off balance. Being pulled off balance is actually easy to recover from physically because there are still a few seconds before I enter the course. But something about being pulled off balance and caught off guard makes me feel slightly out of control, and that messes with my confidence. On the other hand, being ready for the acceleration and not being moved off balance even an inch gives me a sense of being in control and gets my juices flowing as I head into the course.

Just a few seconds later, it is time to make my first cut to set up my jump. I pull out to the left of the boat. Ski boats have a switch on the rope that is connected to the boat's throttle. When you pull the rope, the boat accelerates . . . and hard. Again, if I am not ready, then I will be pulled off balance; but if I am in the right position, then I remain in perfect balance, all the boat's acceleration courses through my body, and I sling up beside the boat. Then from the left side of the boat I make an even harder cut toward the right side of the boat. Crossing behind the boat, I am reaching speeds of fifty or more miles per hour. When I am right behind the boat, that is when I feel the greatest pull. The Chevy 350 is now screaming, and so is the wind in the ear holes of my helmet. As I come up on the right-hand side of the boat, I am the full seventy-five-foot-rope-length away from the boat, but actually I'm twenty or more feet ahead of it. As I slow down, I am preparing to make my final turn to the ramp. At this point, the boat is forty-five feet to the right of the ramp moving thirty-five miles per hour. I am seventy-five feet to the right of the boat or about 120 feet to the right of the ramp with the boat between the ramp and me. It is here, in these critical few moments, that so much happens so fast. Coming into the final turn to the ramp, I ski with what I call "eyes wide open." What I mean by this is that I have to see lots of things at once, knowing how they relate to one another without focusing too hard on any one of them. I have to make adjustments, considering how each aspect will affect my position at the base of the ramp. I love this part because it is so intense and forces me to make instantaneous decisions.

As I come up onto the boat, I am moving faster than the boat is, so there is no rope tension. When I begin my turn, I am still outrunning the boat, so there is still no rope tension. But by the time I finish my turn, I am skiing much slower than the boat. So, when the boat catches up to me, the rope grows tight—when it does, the feeling is like being shot out of a cannon.

You cannot think about it at the time, but every good skier knows that you approach the ramp at around sixty miles per hour. When you hit the ramp, you are going to absorb 3 G's of force for about 0.2 seconds. You have to be in perfect balance. Hitting the ramp is similar to the feeling of jumping off the roof of your house and onto a wet, slimy rock. If you aren't aligned, your feet will fly out from under you or you might come off the ramp upside down. I've seen it happen many times. So you have to both focus and see everything at once, all at the same time. The boat slings you toward the ramp. Your legs are slightly bent, your back is straight, and hopefully you are locked into a strong, well-balanced position.

When you cross behind the boat, the power coming down the rope is so strong that it is not possible to change your position without losing control. You must be ready to hit the ramp before you get there. As you approach the ramp, you allow your body to drift slightly forward, but not too much. You just want your momentum to carry you forward when you kick the ramp. There is a jolt, then a violent lifting. Soon, you are rising in the air, usually nearly three stories high. If the wind is in your face, then you can really lean out over your skis for extra distance. But if it's at your back, leaning too much can cause you to suddenly go straight out beyond your skis and land on your face. All of this is important, and your mind is making a thousand calculations, a thousand corrections, as you fly nearly the length of a football field. If you jump correctly, you can look down to your right and see that you are passing the boat zooming along far below you. It is an odd experience. But then so is soaring three stories up at sixty miles per hour! Finally, you land. There is a crash of water, and you hope you do not splatter yourself awkwardly when you hit.

You want to keep hold of the rope, stay standing if you can, and then prepare for the hard jerk of the rope as the boat races ahead and violently jerks you forward.

So much can go wrong. You can hit the ramp at an odd angle. Your body can be out of alignment. You can allow the tension on the rope to pull you too far forward and thus set you up for a painful crash. Or, you can lose your positioning as you launch into the air, causing you to come down in a tumble and—very likely—end up with a trip to the hospital. Water skiing is a dangerous sport. But I love it.

That doesn't mean, of course, that I've always done it perfectly. Back to my junior year in high school and that year during the regional competition, on my first of three jumps, I came off the ramp with bad timing and worse position. Halfway through the jump, I had turned completely upside down. When I hit the water, my right ski hit my left ankle and slashed it open. Though I made my plea to the judges to continue with the competition, the judges ruled that the injury was too severe for me to continue. There would be many such disappointments in my career.

For the Lord God will help me: therefore shall I not be confounded: therefore have I set my face like a flint, and I know that I shall not be ashamed.

Isaiah 50:7

CARE

Shields of Strength

CHAPTER THREE

SUCCESS NOSEDIVES

By the following summer, though, I had all but forgotten the accident and was focused again on the regional tournament coming up in Baton Rouge, Louisiana. I spent the summer training with all my heart. The discipline and hard work made a difference. A full month before the tournament, I was skiing better than the year before. Coming into the regional competition, I was favored to place first or second, an easy qualifier for the national tournament. But two weeks before the tournament, I took the biggest fall of my short career and broke my left femur (thigh bone) completely in two. I would spend two months in the hospital, the next two years getting the strength back in my leg, and another year catching up to the competition.

By the summer of 1987—a full three years after the broken leg—I was a nineteen-year-old college student, and I was back in shape and skiing better than ever. Every setback seemed to strengthen my resolve and equip me with a better understanding of the obstacles before me. Coming into the regional tournament that year in Dallas, I was at top performance and primed for the championship.

My first jump of the regional tournament was one of my best ever. I felt certain I would place first or second and finally get my chance to compete at the national level. Everything seemed perfect as I pushed off the ramp for the first jump. Then, at the peak of the jump, something went wrong. The tips of my skis dropped, allowing the wind to get on top of the skis. When that happened, both of the ski tips went straight down, immediately causing me to invert. I landed hard on my back and shoulders, and the force of the fall knocked me unconscious. When the rescue swimmers reached me, I was floating face down in the water. As they lifted me up and over to get my face out of the water, I regained consciousness. Somehow I was able to convince the judges I was fine to ski again. But before I could take another jump, I blacked out a second time. It was then, I guess, when I sort of blacked out on my faith, too.

Trust in the Lord with all of your heart and lean not on your own understanding; in all your ways acknowledge Him; and He will make your paths straight.

Proverbs 3:5-6

CHAPTER FOUR

LETTING GO OF FAITH

After the injuries and blackouts, I started believing and accepting that I was a failure. Recounting my struggle up to that point, I saw that every time I reached the top of my game, I would make a poor decision or something would happen to send my hopes plummeting. It seemed as if I had been taking one step forward and two steps back. As discouragement settled over me, I began slowly letting go of my faith—so gradually and subtly that, at first, I didn't realize what was happening.

I think it was the combination of build-ups and let-downs; every time I almost got there, all the wheels came off year after year. I hoped that all my hard work would allow me to finally get to the nationals and that I could redefine myself, and then to land on my head in front of everyone and walk away seeing my name in dead last place again all finally broke my spirit and changed my own way of thinking. From that summer forward, instead of jumping to win or competing with my focus and heart set on being my best, I began a slide into fear of failure. My hope was not to win but merely not to fail again and only reinforce that I was not who I dreamed of being. Instead of hoping my dream would come true, I was just hoping I would not fail again.

When I headed for regionals the next year, I was skiing smarter and better than ever. But spiritually, I wasn't prepared to even get out of bed, much less tackle competition. Instead of expecting to win, I was focused on not failing. I skied without passion, joy, or resolve, shadowed by the fear that I would simply waste another opportunity. That year I won the regionals. I lived the triumph, not as a victory, but as an extension of the fear that had flooded my spirit. Winning, when I was full of fear, was empty and more frightening, I think, than losing. It was great to have the trophy, but my confidence had slipped away so much that part of me could hardly believe that I had actually won. Fear just works that way. It robs you of the joy of victory.

I can remember the national competition in 1988 as if it were yesterday. My good friend Trey and I drove from Beaumont, Texas, to West Palm Beach, Florida, for the tournament. It took us twenty-three hours, and we drove it nonstop. I was scheduled to ski early the next morning. I remember that I experienced the adventure of the road trip—the fulfillment of a part of my dream and the challenge ahead of me—not with elation and excitement, but with a growing sense of dread. I was enduring the event rather than embracing the opportunity. Every mile of the drive seemed to add to my fear of failure.

Once there, I joined more than a thousand of the nation's best skiers, most of them pumped and primed to win. I gauged my chances against other skiers who were twice my size and who exhibited equal or better skills. Most had skied in several national competitions already. My mood sunk lower as my fear rose. I was sure I would lose . . . and so I did. When the competition was over, I had been out-jumped by more than forty feet. I didn't wait for the results. I left the competition site before the tournament was even over, went back to the hotel, loaded up my luggage, and headed home. For ten years, I had fought for a chance to make my dream come true, but when I finally got that chance, I skied so poorly that no one even knew I had shown up.

There had been other losses in my ski career—more losses than wins. Many times before fear began to haunt me, I had been beaten in competition by greater degrees. But those disappointments served only to strengthen my resolve to fight that much harder to win. This time I had not only lost the physical battle; I'd lost the spiritual trial as well by acting on fear instead of faith. The sense of failure was so deep and devastating for me that I felt totally defeated—and I completely gave up skiing.

CHAPTER FIVE

TIME OUT

For the next five years, I never touched my skis. I took all my skiing gear and put it away where I would not have to look at it and be reminded that I had given up. I did what I could to avoid traveling the road that passed the water ski training lake. For the first couple of years, I still received my water ski magazines and other literature. I would always throw them away without looking them over. After two years off the water, I was doing fine and had done a good job of putting most of the memories out of my mind. My only lingering problem came every August when the USA Water Ski Nationals were held. No one needed to tell me it was that time of year. I could feel it in the air. In the south, thunderstorms are very common in the heat of summer. Ski tournaments are often interrupted by storms and the lightning that comes with them.

My fifth year out, I remember being on a trip to south Texas when I stopped for some gas on a desolate highway in the middle of nowhere. After starting the gas pump, I felt the summer heat and noticed a thunderstorm on the horizon. Until that point, I had been excited about the trip and did not even remember that the Water Ski Nationals were in progress. The approaching storm suddenly reminded me of the championship ski competition that was then underway. In that moment, I knew I was out of place and that I should be there. For the rest of the trip, I wrestled with my thoughts. Part of me really missed chasing my dream and wanted to think of being there and winning, but the other part wanted to just forget about it and have a good time on my trip.

In those five years of not skiing, even if I couldn't admit it to myself, my desire to win a national gold medal had not decreased even a little bit. The one thing that had decreased was my confidence that I could win a national championship. This decreased confidence was because I had ended on a fear high, because I had seen my efforts and myself as a failure. I was convinced that I wasn't good enough to win the nationals. I thought I would never ski again.

CHAPTER SIX

TIME IN

By the summer of 1992, everything was looking down. I was five years removed from my chance at my dream, and I had just gone through a breakup with a long-time girlfriend. I was wondering where my life was going. After a Saturday of fishing, I was tired and feeling broken-hearted. Around 9:00 p.m., as I lay on my couch at my apartment, I heard a knock on the patio door. I answered and my little brother, Gabe, walked in all dressed up for a night on the town. He was all smiles, insisting I get up, get dressed, and go out with him and his friends. I was positive that was not going to happen. I got back on the couch and said, "Thanks, but I am in no mood to leave."

For the next thirty minutes, he tried to coax me
into going with him. I never even considered it.
After about forty-five minutes, he went to the
closet, pulled out one of my shirts, and got out my
iron and ironing board. He brought them to the
room I was in and started ironing a shirt for me. I
told him I appreciated his thoughtfulness, but he
was wasting his time. After he finished ironing
the shirt and dousing my carpet with starch, he
pulled out some white jeans, my cowboy hat, my
boots, and a belt from my closet, and told me to
fix my hair. After nearly an hour, he was more
determined than when he walked in the door. The
more I said no, the more determined he became
until I finally agreed to go with him. I had one
condition: as soon as I wanted to come home, we
would come home.

We drove about an hour into Louisiana to a club
called the Longhorn. When I figured out where
we were going, I was really wishing I had stayed
on the couch. Gabe was only trying to help me.
He did not want to see me home sulking and
feeling sorry for myself. But this was looking
like a bad idea, and I was not feeling any better.
Inside the club, everyone seemed to be having
a great time. I took a seat on a bench in the
middle of the crowd and wondered why I had

ever agreed to come here. As I got up to find a quieter place out of the crowd, I saw my former girlfriend there dancing and having what looked to me like a great time. Man, was I ready to leave! "Only my little brother could get me into something like this," I thought. A few minutes later, I found him and told him I was ready to go. He started giving me his "come on have some fun" pitch, and I let him know with some conviction I really was ready to leave.

As we were about to walk out, a girl whom I had noticed earlier walked by us. I told Gabe to look at her, that I had seen her across the dance floor earlier that night. I thought she seemed out of place. She was beautiful—or "fine" as we say in southeast Texas. I was sure that she was too good looking to notice me, and she looked too proper for a stranger in a cowboy hat to approach. Besides, I was in no mood to talk to a girl anyway. I should never have said all this to Gabe. He started pushing me in her direction and urging me to ask her to dance. I told him the last thing I needed on my way out was for a girl to tell me she did not want to dance with me. The more I argued with him, the more adamant he was.

Finally, I made it really clear that I was leaving, I was not asking her to dance, and I was through with our conversation. Through, that is, until he told me that if I did not ask her to dance, he would. Now, I knew full well that Gabe had a way with the girls and that if he asked her to dance, he would get that dance. I told him to wait right where he was. I went over to her and introduced myself. She told me her name was Tammie. I was expecting something like hello or good evening or some fancy greeting. When I asked her if she would like to dance, she said, "Sure." Wouldn't you know it; the first song we danced was a slow song. It was even longer than usual because the song was played more than once. After that, we danced four or five songs straight. By the end of the night, I had mustered enough courage to ask Tammie for her phone number and also to ask her what she was doing the next day. She said she was going to the beach with some of her friends. Of course I said, "So am I!" I got her phone number and she left. I saw Gabe a few minutes later, and the first thing he did was ask if I had gotten the "digits." He meant her phone number. And I had.

All the way home I was on cloud nine. Gabe and I went to the beach the next day, and it took all day for me to find Tammie and her friends. After

32

a short visit, everyone was going home, so just before we all left, I asked her if she wanted to go to a movie. She took me up on the invitation, and we went out with my sister and her boyfriend the same night. After the movie, I took Tammie home, and we sat for hours on her parents' couch, talking about everything.

It wasn't long after that Tammie and I started seeing each other on a regular basis and getting to know each other better, and the subject of my skiing came up. I was surely not going to tell her I had quit due to fear, so I told her I was just burned out. She asked me if she could see me ski, and I wanted to impress her. When I called my old ski coach, he told me to come on out to his property and jump. It was "that pride thing" that had first gotten me up on the skis, to make sure I kept up with my sister, and I guess it was a bit of "that pride thing" that made me want Tammie to see me ski and jump. Many times fear follows closely on the heels of pride, and I would later have to turn that pride over to God in order to be free of the fear. Anyway, one trip to the lake led to another, and before I knew it, I was skiing regularly again.

During my ski-less five-year stint I had spent a lot of time in the gym, and the workouts had added twenty pounds of muscle to my frame. I was stronger than I had ever been, and the added strength improved my skiing. In three months, I was skiing at a level much higher than before I had quit. It also helped that Paul Merrill, a twenty-five-year veteran of Cypress Gardens and a repeat national champion, was spending the summer with my coach, so I had two fine men training me to be my best. Everything seemed to be going great. In an effort to keep the fear of failure from creeping in and taking over, I decided that if I did get to compete at nationals again, I would not expect to win. I thought that if I accepted the idea that I was not capable of winning I would not have to worry about the fear of failing.

I must stop here and say this: never take that attitude! God only knows how many of His champions have lived their lives with this attitude stifling their potential, killing their dreams, and limiting God's plan for them. Adopting an attitude that embraces failure or leaves your dream to fate is really just another way of giving up. When you begin to believe that you can never become a champion, that you can never overcome something in your life, you may face less fear because you are accepting defeat before you even have a chance to live your destiny. That is the opposite of what God has planned for your life, and take it from me, the one thing that is worse than fighting fearfully is knowing you are no longer in the fight because of fear. Your goal should be to fight all things with power, love, and a sound mind, but if you can't do that, then at least fight.

As long as you are in the fight, even if you are fighting scared, God can get you where He needs you. The Bible says in John 10:10, "The devil comes only to steal and to kill and destroy; I have come that you may have life, and have it more abundantly." In Jeremiah 29:11, God says, "For I know the plans I have for you, plans to prosper you, not to harm you, plans to give you a future and a hope." How can we justify pride or fear when we read those statements? When we can see our lives as more about God than about ourselves, it's kind of hard to concede defeat in any situation. A trial is just a footpath to walk with God. A challenge is just an opportunity to hold His hand more tightly. The element of loss is fleeting for those who walk in faith. We may not know how He will make it work, but if we have faith, we know He will make every setback work for our good if we follow His lead. Then we can consider adversity an incredible adventure with God.

> "And we know that God causes all things to work together for good to those who love God, to those who are called according to His purpose."
> —*Romans 8:28*

A new heart also will I give you, and a new spirit will I put within you.

Ezekiel 36:26

AFC

Shields of Strength

CHAPTER SEVEN

GIVING IT UP

My first year back as a competitor, I placed third in the regionals again, and for the second time in my life, I qualified for nationals. But qualifying was about all I did. When I got to the national tournament in West Palm Beach, Florida, I couldn't help but hope that I would at least win a medal. But as soon as I decided to hope, I was suddenly reminded of all the fear and failure of my last national competition experience.

The night before the competition, I hardly slept. Every hour I would wake up to check the clock to see if it was time to get up and get ready to ski. Maybe this time I had a real chance to place in the top three. That hope wrestled with my fear of messing up again. The speed, skill, and timing called for in a national ski competition require a sound mind. A focus on fear overrides the possibility of a sound mind.

In my performance that year, there was no question that hope lost the battle. In short, I skied horribly. The performance wasn't the result of a bad break or chance circumstances but of my conscious decision to act on fear. Both times that I had been given the chance to make my dream come true, I couldn't keep my wits about me long enough to follow through. I felt, each time, like I had thrown the dream overboard. The worst realization to me was that I really didn't have the heart of a champion. I couldn't face the competition head on, couldn't rally to the challenge, and couldn't make my hard work, expertise, determination, and desire stand up against my fear. My perception was built on my control, not God's; on my potential and fallibility, not God's love and power and faithfulness; on my glory, not God's. Soon, though, I learned that God can change hearts if we let Him.

For we wrestle not
against flesh and blood,
but against principalities,
against powers, and
against the rulers of
darkness of the world.
Ephesians 6:12

Shields of Strength

CHAPTER EIGHT

TAKING IT BACK

The next year I had a plan. Through discipline, hard work, and mind power, I was going to beat the fear. I trained extra hard, skiing a minimum of five days a week. Tammie made sure that every training session I had was videotaped, and I reviewed my videos every night without fail. I would look for any missteps or mistakes and visualize every way to make the jumps better, faster, farther. That year at regionals in Austin, Texas, I won the competition. So far, the hard work and discipline were paying off. Still, I wanted to leave as little as possible to chance. I planned to arrive at the national tournament site—it was held at West Palm Beach again—two days early so I could practice on the lake and ramp. I figured the extra time would allow me to familiarize myself with my competition and the surroundings. Surely that would diminish my fear and anxiety.

Once at the competition site, I met the fear I had been trying to dodge. All the hard work, the discipline, and the careful plans didn't shield me from the fear. In fact, all my hard work did not even faze the fear. I felt more afraid than ever before. That year, up to that point, I had skied for six months straight—more than six hundred jumps without a crash. But in Thursday's tournament practice, with fear robbing me of a sound mind, I crashed on my second jump. On Friday, I took to the lake for one last practice set, and I crashed on my first jump.

The following day was the day I would compete in the nationals, and Friday's practice proved a good predictor of how I would do in the competition. My first two jumps were only 135 feet each, and though I had no certainty of how far my jumps were at the time, I knew as I executed them that neither was good enough to win. When it came time for my last jump, I was in a total state of panic. I decided to forget about everything I had been taught to do and on my last jump build as much speed as possible and attack the ramp with or without control. That mindset is one of the best ways to get hurt in my sport, and though I knew this in my heart, somehow the pain of an injury seemed easier to swallow than the humiliation and pain of fear and failure. On that last jump I did everything wrong, but I did manage to keep from crashing. The jump was enough to put me in third place. But I knew I had skied poorly and that I had moved through the competition that day as if I were living out a bad dream. It is a nightmare to be so totally without confidence and faith and to be consumed with such a smothering dread of failure.

Even though I took home the bronze that year, I knew I had skied poorly in a heavy cloak of fear that weighed me down, kept me from doing the best I could do, and robbed me of any joy in winning. I remember walking away from the lake, still wrapped up in my fear, as the U.S. team coach approached me to tell me that my last jump had moved me into third place. I told him, "Jay, I need to come ski with you. I need some help bad." And even though Jay Bennett is the finest ski jump coach I know, I knew even then that I needed more than he could offer. The truth was that something was pulling me down, something that physical training and technique couldn't counter.

Physical training and preparation are a must, and I would not have had a chance with or without the fear if I had not trained so hard. Still, it was becoming clear that physical might was no match for the battle I was fighting against fear and failure. Gradually, I was beginning to understand that I needed more than physical training to win. The battle I was losing was spiritual.

CHAPTER NINE

PERSEVERING

In 1996, I would qualify again for nationals by skiing the best I had ever skied. In most of my practice sets, I was jumping far enough already to win the national tournament. Tammie had seen the fear I was fighting. She knew the fear never left me when I skied. She also knew that I needed to learn that God's Word, not my hard work, would get me through the fear. Tammie and her mom were strong Christians who knew God's Word and knew how to pray. Thankfully, they both understood spiritual battles. Tammie had been raised by her mom and dad reading and understanding God's Word. She understood something that I had never considered, and this was that overcoming fear was a spiritual battle that could not be won by just becoming better at what I do. It was a battle that could only be won with faith and in finding a way to act on God's Word no matter what.

I loved the Lord, but I did not know His Word, and I did not believe I should be asking the Lord for anything unless it meant life or death. It had never even crossed my mind to ask the Lord to help me overcome my fear; or, that it could be that God Himself had already left me His Word with all the power to help me function with the heart of a champion instead of fear. What I did know, though, was that no one loved me more than Tammie, and I could see an amazing power inside her. There was a courage in Tammie that could stand in circumstances that would make most grown men faint. She was so sweet and pretty, but the more I got to know her, the more I began to realize that special strength that faith and God's Word had built within her. The funny thing was I knew I needed what she had but had no idea how to get it.

Tammie was the first girl I had ever met that I found myself going to for advice about my own fears and failures. I didn't go to Tammie because she had all the answers. Heck, most of the things

I went to her about weren't really things anyone could have an answer to anyway. She, like most of my good friends, would encourage me, but unlike any friend I had ever had, she would also share with me scriptures that applied to my problems. Sometimes she would just encourage me because she just didn't know what scripture would apply. Then a day or two later I would get a card from her with more encouragement and a few scriptures she had found that applied to my problem. Each one of those few scriptures would touch my heart in ways that words alone never could, and before long I was starting to realize there was much more to this God thing than I had ever realized.

I wanted more of what Tammie had but did not know how to ask her, so I called my uncle, Richard Vaughan, who was a pastor. I didn't really know Uncle Richard very well because the only time I ever talked to him was at Thanksgiving every year. But he was the pastor of the family, and I thought I could tell him about what I saw in Tammie and perhaps he could guide me as to how to have what she had. I told my uncle all about her over the phone, and he invited me over for a steak so we could get into the Bible and see what it said. That sounded great to me.

I believed the Bible was God's Word, and I wanted to know what it had to say about all this. Uncle Richard spent about two hours with me just showing me scriptures and what the Bible said about prayer, faith, and the power of God's Word. He explained to me how I could have what Tammie had and showed me what the Bible said about what I wanted. Best of all, he helped me see in God's Word what Christ really came for, why He died on the cross, and how everything Christ had done was so I could receive everything I was looking for. He showed me scriptures from the Bible that allowed me to understand that Tammie's peace and strength were a free gift from God that was also available to me if I would just give my heart to Christ. That night my life changed forever when I gladly made the decision to receive my Lord into my heart, but my journey to learning to live from my new heart had only just begun. Tammie and I started attending Uncle Richard's church the very next Sunday. I knew I had a lot to learn and that it was going to take awhile.

Most of that year I prayed God would help me with my fear. I quoted scriptures constantly. I was trying to get in shape spiritually. Uncle Richard, Tammie, and Tammie's mom were doing a good job of teaching me how to develop a relationship with the Lord, how to learn and apply His Word, and how to listen to the Lord. I was doing everything I knew how to do to overcome my fear of ski competition, including praying while I skied. Nothing seemed to make a difference.

As the weeks moved me closer to the competition, Tammie continued to watch me struggle with my fear. One day when I showed up to ski, I noticed something written in red on my ski handle. I had always written the one or two things my coaches told me would make the biggest difference in my jumping on my handle so I would not forget them and would be constantly reminded to apply them. I had just bought a new handle, though, and had not had time to write my new tips on it yet. Tammie had commandeered my handle before I could write my technique tips on it and had written two scriptures on it instead. She wrote Philippians 4:13, which said, "I can do all things through Christ who strengthens me," and II Timothy 1:7, which says, "For God has not given me the spirit of fear but of power, of love and of a sound mind." When I read those two scriptures, it was the first time I had ever heard either of them. I can't even tell you how much it meant to me to know God's Word said that. I am telling you, that girl was persistent in her love for me and her desire to help me become a champion. She was doing more to get me there than any coach I had ever worked with.

At the three-week countdown before the national championship, I knew I was skiing well enough to win, but the fear was still shadowing me. In my heart, I didn't really want to work so hard only to fail again. The thought of sleepless nights added to the fear. To make matters even worse, just two weeks before the nationals when I was training and pushing really hard to get those few extra feet I knew I would need in a couple of weeks if I were going to have a chance to win, I made a terrible mistake and hit the ramp with my chest too low. I was slightly bent forward when I hit the ramp, and the result was a headfirst crash. Tammie even got this one on video. It was really ugly. Although I did not receive any injuries that required a hospital visit, I did receive more minor injuries in this one crash than I had ever experienced before.

Still shots taken from the actual video of the crash.

That night after the crash I was lying on my couch and Tammie was packing the ice on me. I had pulled my thigh muscle and my groin, partially dislocated my shoulder, and sprained my ankle and my wrist. My helmet had been smashed down on my head so hard that it cut my cheek and put a goose egg just above my right eye, and I had bruised a rib. Lying on the couch, I started thinking about how I still had not overcome my fear. I looked at myself with my face all beat up and several body parts swollen. I started asking myself, "What the heck are you doing?" The more I thought, the more I started to think maybe I was not too smart, maybe I was striving for something I would never achieve. I asked Tammie to come sit by me as I was lying on the couch with all my ice packs. I told her I was going to quit. I could always tell that it hurt Tammie worse than it hurt me every time I got hurt, and after seeing how upset she was about this crash, I really thought she was going to say "THANK GOD." Instead she started crying and saying, "You can't quit. I can't believe after all you have gone through you would quit now. You're not going to quit, Kenny. You can win the nationals. You can do anything you want. You can do all things through Christ who strengthens you. Please don't quit. You can do it." Seeing her confidence in me and her faith to believe, even when I was lying there looking like a fool, kept me in the game. I promised Tammie I would not quit and got back on the water as soon as possible.

For most of my life, if you had asked me what perseverance is, I would have told you it is all about never quitting no matter what. Maybe you have heard that a quitter never wins and a winner never quits. What I had to learn was that, in the really tough challenges, sometimes it is impossible to never quit. Sometimes things are just so bad that all you can do in the moment is lie down and give up. What I have now learned is that perseverance is not about never quitting. There are even times that giving up is the best answer to ensure your perseverance. Sometimes the injury, loss, or hopelessness causes even the strongest among us to quit. The difference in those who persevere and those who do not isn't not quitting; it is finding the courage to get back up as quickly as possible. When you feel as though you just can't go another inch or stand another moment of despair, maybe you need to quit so you can start over tomorrow with more determination than ever and with God by your side. Not persevering, in my opinion, is when you still have the dream and desire in your heart but decide you will never try again. If you can't get back up on your own, then let someone else help you. Your destiny does not depend on whether you ever quit; it depends on whether or not you ultimately find the courage to get back up.

So I got back to my training, and it was while I was driving home from a training session one day that God met me. I was in my truck, and I remember thinking that I was skiing well enough to place in the nationals, but I also had to admit to myself that if I had not made a commitment to Tammie and my coach, I would not have even gone to the nationals. I knew I was still too plagued by fear. Frankly, I had simply come to accept that I was incapable of overcoming fear. I knew it, to the core of my being, and I also knew that there was not a thing I could do about it. Right then, at that moment of complete awareness of my weakness, I felt some words impressed on my heart. Some people would say God spoke, and others would say they just remembered the words of the Bible. I don't know and it doesn't matter. I can tell you this: in that moment, this is what I heard and this is what happened to my heart. The words were these: "You're not incapable. You're a son of the King of Kings. My Word says if you ask and believe you've received, then go out and act on what you've been given. Quit looking back over your shoulder to see if I'm with you. Change the way you pray from asking to thanking." Right then, right there, the fear that had dominated me left. It was just no longer there. God had reached into my soul and torn that torturing enemy right out of me. It was a miracle.

I cast down imaginations, and every high thing that exalteth itself against the knowledge of God, and bring into captivity every thought to the obedience of Christ. II Corinthians 10:5

CHAPTER TEN

THE STARTING DOCK

The next week's training went very well, and by the end of it I was headed for Fort Walton Beach, Florida, for the national championship competition. Tammie and I drove this trip since it was only about an eight-hour drive. She was supposed to help me stay awake on the trip, but Tammie cannot stay awake in a car, so she was sleeping before we crossed the Louisiana state line. She asked me to wake her up at each state line so she could see the welcome signs on the highway. When we made Louisiana, I woke her up, and she looked up for a minute, said, "Thank you, and make sure you wake me up when we get to the next state line." I thought, *I guess that means I am driving this one alone.* When we got to Mississippi, I woke her up, and she again looked up, slurred a thank you, said she was sorry, and went right back to sleep. When we crossed into Alabama, she did the same thing. Finally, when we crossed the Florida state line, she felt so bad for sleeping the whole way she managed to stay awake for the last hour of the drive. I think she just wanted to see the beaches.

This would not be a year I would spend much time taking in the tournament talk at the starting dock. The starting dock at a ski tournament is like the water cooler in the office. At nationals, the conversation shared at the starting dock can be valuable and useful. Sometimes, though, the dialogue takes a downturn as folks make excuses for not overcoming their fears. I have been known to indulge in this kind of conversation myself, but more often I have found the discussions more distracting than beneficial. The conversation usually goes something like this:

"Man, that boat driver is horrible!"

"The wind is up one minute and down the next . . ."

"The ramp is so fast you can't keep your balance!"

"That water is so slow it kills your timing."

"That boat makes a huge wake."

"They must have just put on a new rope.
It's like a rubber band."

"The sun is a killer coming into the ramp!"

And so on . . .

That year, I felt my energy would best be spent in prayer, practice, and action—focusing on God's Word and my training—rather than hanging around the starting dock. I had trained for every condition, and I was not going to sit around and listen to things that would distract me or fill me with fear. If there really was a problem, I would know it, and with a sound mind, I could adjust for it.

I share this because no matter what you do, you can find a "starting dock" where everybody who knows everything about what you do can share an endless string of negative comments that present problems without proposed solutions. I say find a good starting dock buzzing with talk about overcoming, never giving up, and never failing through Christ. When this is the conversation around the water ski starting dock, I hang around. Apart from the ski competition circuit, good starting docks for life's challenges can exist in good churches and with good Christian friends and fellowship.

CHAPTER ELEVEN

NO WAY TO LOSE

The next day was the big day. The same old challenges began to line up like skiers in a competition. Resting that night offered the usual struggle for a short time, but then I managed to fall into a deep sleep that lasted through the night. I woke up early and felt well rested. At the waterfront, my warm-up went smoothly. I would be skiing as the fifth seed, or fifth from the last contender in the line of sixty or so jumpers. The number-one-ranked skier competes last in the lineup, so that meant there were only four skiers ranked higher than I was.

During the day I had to choke back my fear several times. Tammie was by my side the whole time, and she kept reminding me to stay focused on God's Word. Over and over, she kept telling me she knew I would do well. She told me she believed in me and felt the Lord was with me. Each time fear came creeping into my thoughts, I would focus on God's Word, but I was still battling. II Corinthians 10:5 says "Cast down imaginations and every high thing that exalts itself against the knowledge of God and bring into captivity every thought to the obedience of Christ." In other words, even though God had delivered me from my fear, it did not mean that I would not be tempted to be fearful again and again. The key to keeping my sound mind was to keep casting down negative and distracting thoughts and to continue thinking about God's Word instead.

When the lineup got down to the top ten skiers, I knew I was still in the running because no one had beaten my best distance. A skier's rank is based solely on his average performance in a certain number of tournaments. Sometimes skiers have a few bad tournaments and end up ranked lower than they should be. All the top athletes know one another, and we know who is skiing the best, regardless of ranking. That day I knew that if anyone would jump farther than I could, it would be Lyle Perkins, the skier skiing just before me. However, by the time he had made two of his three jumps, he still had not taken the lead. As he took his last jump, I was putting on my knee brace. I heard him hit the ramp, and then I heard the crowd break out in excited cheers and loud applause. As I put on the rest of my equipment, I heard the announcer report his distance. He had taken over first place with a 173-foot jump—five feet farther than I had ever jumped.

Tammie helped me pull my speed suit on before she left to video my jumps from a better perch. After hearing Lyle's distance, she told me I could do all things through Christ who strengthens me. She told me she knew I could do it and not to worry about how far Lyle jumped because she knew I could jump farther. As I pulled my skis on, I started to think, *I can't believe it! I am one jump away from being able to take over the lead and maybe have my dream come true, and this guy jumps five feet farther than my personal best.* Those thoughts seemed to bring the fear back in full force. Just at that moment, though, I remembered II Timothy 1:7: "For God has not given me the spirit of fear, but of power, of love, and of a sound mind." I knew I needed to concentrate harder on God's Word. Then I had this thought, *I am just going to do the best I can for Jesus and not worry about winning.* As I made that decision, I realized that I would do more for the Lord than I would for a gold medal or trophy anyway. Best of all, I knew if I gave God my best until I was finished He would not be disappointed in me. It was a higher calling with no chance of failing. For the first time in my life, in that moment, I took my focus off the gold medal and my dream and put it on God and doing the best I could for Him. Sometime after this important day in my life, I discovered the scripture for what God had led me to do. It was Matthew 6:33: "But seek you first the kingdom of God and His righteousness and all these things will be added unto you."

In all things I am
more than a conqueror
through Christ who
loves me.

AFC

Romans 8:37

Shields
of Strength

CHAPTER TWELVE

No Way to Win

My first jump was 172 feet—four feet farther
than my personal best but still one foot
short of the leader. On my second attempt, my
timing was off. As I finished making my turn for
the final approach to the ramp, I realized I was
running behind and I might not get on the ramp.
Because I am coming to the ramp from an angle
that is right to left, if I start my cut too late, I will
hit the side of the ramp instead of the bottom.
As you can imagine, that is not a good thing. I
know that if I am headed for the side of the ramp
I must let go of the rope and ski around the ramp.
On the other hand, if I do get on, it may be a
great jump because I have to cut very hard to get
there, and as a result if I do make it, I will have

extra speed and possibly a great jump. The really tough decisions come when you are not sure if you will get on or not and when you need a big jump in a big tournament.

This was nationals and I needed the biggest jump of my career. If it is not a big competition, then you don't risk it and you let go of the rope. This time, though, it was going to be really close. It didn't look good, but in the split second I had to make up my mind, and knowing I had to jump farther than I ever had, I just could not make myself let go of the rope. The closer I got to the ramp, the more I began to realize I would not make it. But it was too late to let go. Worst of all, this was exactly how I landed myself in the hospital for two months a few years before. This time, when I hit the ramp, my left ski got on the bottom surface of the ramp, but my right ski did not make it and hung off the side of the ramp. I am telling you that is such a bad place to be that it is hard for me to even say it. Imagine one ski on the ramp and one off at nearly seventy miles per hour.

I had learned some lessons from my crash a few years back, so I instantly allowed my legs to collapse in an attempt to stay low and hopefully prevent an injury. Still, I had felt my right ski hang on the side of the ramp. That threw me off balance. I lost control and crashed. Both skis came off in the water. I wasn't hurt, but when I came to rest in the water, I could see I had ripped the fin off the bottom of my right ski. I always carry a spare fin and a battery-powered hand screwdriver for just such an emergency. In ski competition, a skier has three minutes to repair any kind of equipment damage or failure. If the repairs are not finished within the three minutes, the judges call a forced forfeit.

I handed my skis to the boat crew and then climbed onto the platform on the back of the boat, grabbed a handle near the rear of the boat, and held on tight as the boat driver put the hammer down and rushed me back to the starting dock where I could replace the broken fin with a new one. Just as the boat took off, I heard someone yelling my name from the shore. I looked up and noticed that one of my competitors was holding up a fin while running as fast as he could toward the starting dock. He was still at least a thousand feet from the dock but was running with all his might. It was Jeff Latimer, a national competitor of many years from Alabama. He had noticed I hit the side of the ramp and saw my fin shatter on the ramp. He was afraid I didn't have another fin and was doing all he could to help make sure I did not lose my last jump. Something about seeing him wanting me to win helped keep my spirits high for just those few seconds and helped me refocus. I did have a spare fin, so I just yelled back to Jeff that I had one, but I will never forget seeing him running with his hand high in the air, showing me he had a fin for my ski if I needed it and knowing that if I landed a good jump it would only bump Jeff down in the standings. What a great guy!

As soon as I got to the dock, I worked as quickly as I could and managed to secure the new fin. As soon as I had the last screw tightened, I heard the judge's voice over the boat radio announcing that my time was up. I let them know immediately that I was ready and hurriedly began to put my skis back on. I pulled my left ski on first. Then as I slid my foot into the right ski, I noticed the boot felt way too loose. Tight boots allow a skier more control. Competition skiers wear their ski boots so tight they have to lubricate them with soap to even slide their feet into them. My heart dropped when I saw that the right boot was torn. I hadn't noticed it after the crash because my skis had come off during the fall. Now, there was no more time for repairs.

The boat took off and I was up and on my way to set up for my third and final jump of the competition. These thoughts crowded my consciousness and threatened to make the remainder of the day hopelessly dark: *It's over. I did my best, and I almost made it. At least I can probably count on having second place wrapped up . . . I overcame my fear and jumped four feet farther than my personal best. But now my concentration is broken, and, worst of all, my boot is torn. I'll have to settle for second place because there is no way I can make the jump I need to win with a torn boot. No one can do that.*

The boat was making its final turn to start the approach to the ramp when the Lord reminded me that I had committed to do the best I could for Him. I knew that until I had taken that third and final jump, I had not finished doing the best I could for the Lord. No matter what the circumstances and regardless of the torn boot—I could still do my best until I was finished. As I headed for the ramp, I remembered the scripture on my ski rope handle, the scripture Tammie had written there to help me overcome my fear. Yes, I can do all things through Christ who strengthens me. OK, then. I would continue on with a clear head and do the best I could with the torn boot.

If I was out of control, I could refuse the ramp, let go of the rope, and ski around, but at least I would have acted on God's Word until I finished.

But things got worse. When I made my first cut to set up my approach to the ramp, I cut out too soon. It is very hard to start out too early or too late and make all the corrections I need to make in order to get my timing right before I hit the ramp. If I can't correct a too-early start, I won't have enough speed to make a long jump. Any other time before that day, I'm certain I would have panicked because of my poor timing on such a critical jump, even without the torn boot. But this time I remember calmly thinking that I knew how to correct the situation. To get my timing on track, I needed to make a long, slow turn and pull as hard as I could to get farther past the boat. I remember that as I pulled up beside the boat, I was riding my skis as flat as possible and staying as low as possible, trying to delay my timing.

As I made my final turn to the ramp, I knew all my weight would be on my right ski—the ski with the torn boot. In order to prevent my foot from slipping, I shoved my foot to the right side of the boot and kept constant pressure on that foot all the way to the ramp. It seemed that each small wave, wind, lean, motion, and movement on my part was critical. All the odds were against me even completing this jump. Odds were great that I would be injured, and odds were almost nil that this last jump could possibly be a winning jump. I knew that if I eased up or bounced on the water at all, my foot would slip. And I knew that in order to adjust my timing, I needed to execute the turn . . . slower . . . slower . . . but not too slow. As I finished the turn, I sensed my timing was still too early. From the completion of the last turn until I make contact with the ramp, it is only about three seconds. In those three seconds, my speed accelerates from about ten miles an hour to almost seventy miles an hour.

CHAPTER THIRTEEN

THE VICTORY

In the past, I would have totally succumbed to the fear and lost my sound mind. All my logical reasoning told me that my last jump was doomed for failure. My poor timing and speed were against me. The torn boot alone would make a winning jump impossible. All three factors combined set up odds too stiff for anyone to overcome. But within the critical three seconds—as the boat shot me forward to sixty miles per hour—the unthinkable, unlikely, impossible began to take hold. With as clear and as sound a mind as I have ever had, I was able to tap into everything I had learned over my years of training. I took as long as I could in the turn without taking too long. I was still too early, so I started slowly and pulled harder as I approached the ramp. Halfway to the ramp I knew that I had finally gotten my timing on track but that I did not have enough speed. I pulled as hard as I could to generate as much speed as possible while also making sure I kept my right foot shoved hard into the right side of the torn boot.

When I reached the ramp, I was sure I still did not have enough speed, and I knew I would need to kick the ramp as hard as I could to get extra height and make up for the loss of speed. I executed the kick and timing perfectly, and I am certain that God performed a miracle at that point because I went straight up without slipping one bit. Sailing through the air, halfway through the jump, I realized that my dream had just come true. My last jump was 179 feet—eleven feet farther than my personal best—and distance enough to win the nationals by seven feet!

After I got my skis off, I took off running to find Tammie in the crowd near the jump. When I found her, she was crying. She hugged me and told me how proud she was of me. I asked her what was wrong, and she said she had been strong in front of me, but when she walked away to go video my jumps, she had started crying. She said she was afraid for me because she knew I would have to jump so far to win. She said she knew I could do it, but she was worried I wouldn't. She had been

Still shots taken from the actual video of winning the jump.

crying and praying the whole time. I could not wait to tell her what had been happening in my heart during that competition.

As we began the long drive home, I began sharing with Tammie how the Lord had been working in my spirit as I struggled through those three jumps and how much boldness He had given me. Before we got to the Florida state line, I noticed she was not responding. I left her alone and let her sleep the whole way. I did not need any help to stay awake. I wore my gold medal the whole way home. I relived everything a hundred times and cried every time. I thanked the Lord so many times for all He had done for me. And another thing became very clear to me on my way home: I would need Tammie in my life forever.

I started saving for a ring, and on December 24, 1996, I told Tammie I wanted her to come to church with me and go to the altar so we could pray together and thank God for everything that had happened that year. Uncle Richard opened up the church, and we went and prayed together at the altar. When she got up, I stayed on my knees and asked her to be my wife. She accepted, thank God, and we were married the following May.

Kenny with his first bass.

Kenny learns to ride at an early age.

Kenny's father in his twenties.
Kenny later learned to jump at the same ski club.

The Vaughan children learning to jump. (From top: Bonnie, Kenny, and Gabe)

Hard landing after a long training jump.

Kenny leaving the ramp during a training session at his home lake.

Kenny poses with Dan Coufal, the official announcer at the 1996
Nationals in Fort Walton Beach, Florida.

Kenny celebrates with his wife, Tammie, and long-time coach
Charlie after winning the gold medal.

As a National champion, Kenny is asked to speak
about his experiences across the country.

Where it all began. Pictured here is the tow rope handle
that Tammie inscribed with the scripture that inspired Kenny to
act on his faith to win the gold medal above. Also pictured is
the broken fin that nearly cost Kenny his dream and that
he now keeps as a trophy.

Kenny's parents, Robert and Alice Vaughan

Kenny with his family. From left to right: Tammie, Kennedy, Kenny, Faith, and Grace.

Kenny gears up at the starting dock.

Kenny takes a break from another long day of training.

Faith is ready to hit the water

Grace skiing

Kennedy

Lieutenant Colonel Dodd poses with his wife Sharon and two daughters, Caitlin and Grace, before departing for Afghanistan.

Lieutenant Colonel Dean Triebel gave his last Shield of Strength to Oliver North, when this picture was taken in Iraq.

Major General Hylton gives Kenny a Coin of Excellence
for donating Shields of Strength to his soldiers before
they deployed to Afghanistan.

The members of the 86th Signal Battalion pictured
here with their Shields of Strength were among the first
troops deployed to Afghanistan.

Lieutenant Colonel Dodd, Secretary of the Army Les Brownlee, Kenny, and Lieutenant Colonel Joe Rippetoe at the Pentagon.

Captain Russel Rippetoe—homecoming king, Eagle Scout, captain of the football team, Army Ranger, and Iraqi war hero—was killed in action on April 3rd, 2003. He is pictured here (center) with his family.

Secretary of the Army Les Brownlee looks at Captain Russel Rippetoe's Bible, dog tags, Shields of Strength, and a note from Captain Rippetoe's father. All of these items were with Captain Rippetoe when he was killed in action.
Picture taken at the Pentagon.

After losing a comrade and close friend in battle, Lance Corporal Chris Hankins is baptized in a makeshift basin of plastic-covered boxes wearing a Shield of Strength.

This memorial for nine Marines and one translator is a silent reminder of the price of freedom.

10th Mountain Division
United States Army

2002 USA
Waterski Nationals

National Aeronautics and Space
Administration

Special Warfare
Group 2 Navy Seals

All for One
United States Army

1st Infantry Division
United States Army

25th Infantry Division
United States Army

1st Cavalry Division
United States Army

75th Ranger Regiment
3rd Ranger Battalion United States
Army

US Nuclear Security

United States Army

82nd Airborne Division
United States Army

Firefighter Shield

Unit Ministry Team
3rd Infantry Division

US Naval Academy Headquarters

Walter Reed Army
Medical Center

86th Signal Battalion
United States Army

Camp Willow Run

3rd Infantry Division
United States Army

The shields pictured here were custom made.
For more information about Shields of Strength or to request a catalog,
go to www.shieldsofstrength.com.

CHAPTER FOURTEEN

IN VICTORY'S WAKE

I am here to tell you that overcoming fear is about making a conscious decision to think and act on God's Word. Yes, I did need my physical preparation and all the training. Physically, I was prepared, and that was very important. However, until I got spiritually prepared, I could never have accomplished my dream. All the physical training in the world cannot help you overcome a spiritual battle with fear. But God has already overcome fear for us if we will simply act on His Word in any and all circumstances. When I made a decision to act on God's Word spiritually, I picked up the shield of faith and the sword of the spirit, which enabled me to function with a sound mind. Ephesians 6 says it like this:

Be strong with the Lord's mighty power. Put on all of God's armor so that you will be able to stand firm against all strategies and tricks of the devil. For we are not fighting against people made of flesh and blood, but against the evil rulers and authorities of the unseen world, against those mighty powers of darkness who rule this world, and against wicked spirits in the heavenly realms. Use every piece of God's armor to resist the enemy in the time of evil, so that after the battle you will be standing firm. Stand your ground, putting on the sturdy belt of truth and the body armor of God's righteousness. For shoes, put on the peace that comes from the Good News, so that you will be fully prepared. In every battle you will need faith as your shield to stop the fiery arrows aimed at you by Satan. Put on salvation as your helmet, and take the sword of the spirit, which is the Word of God. Pray at all times and on every occasion in the power of the Holy Spirit.

What I learned has made a difference in how I have lived each day since.

The truth is my fear was never a physical problem. It was a spiritual problem. My fear was coming from an evil power. Putting it plainly and simply, fear was trying to prevent me from functioning with a sound mind. Recognizing the real battle was one critical step for me. Understanding how to fight it was another. For years, I fought the fear with my own effort until I could not fight anymore. Then I gave up, but fortunately God did not give up on me, and the solution was much simpler than I had ever dreamed. All I had to do was act on God's Word, no matter my circumstances. If you think about it, every time the devil tempted the Lord, Jesus would simply quote scripture, and the devil would flee. I figured if Jesus used God's Word to run off the devil, then so should I. However, just quoting scripture is not enough on its own. It wasn't until I decided to act on God's Word that I overcame my fear.

The good news is that we do not have to fight Satan. All we need to do is what God has already told us to do in Ephesians 6—we need to pick up the shield of faith and the sword of the spirit. As I said before, II Corinthians 10:5 says we should cast down imaginations and every high thing that exalts itself against the knowledge of God and bring into captivity every thought to the obedience of Christ. Ephesians 6 is talking about the same high thing, and God is telling us that to overcome the devil, all we need to do is cast out of our minds thoughts of fear and act on God's Word.

The next question is this: What are "thoughts obedient to Christ"? The answer can be found in Philippians 4:8, which reads: "Finally, brothers, whatever is true, whatever is noble, whatever is right, whatever is pure, whatever is lovely, whatever is admirable—if anything is excellent or praiseworthy—think about such things. Whatever you have learned or received or heard from me, or seen in me—put it into practice. And the God of peace will be with you." Now, when I am struck with a thought or thoughts that do not line up with what God's Word says, I make a conscious decision to think and act, not on those thoughts, but on God's Word instead. I continue striving to make decisions based on what God says, not what circumstances or fear might lead me to think. I do this because I have realized God's Word is good for me and is truer than anything I see or feel anyway.

Leading up to those final moments at the national competition, all I could feel in my heart and hear in my mind was defeat. Looking at my situation, defeat was the only outcome that made sense. But by faith, I decided to act on God's Word. When I did that, I allowed God to work in me to overcome my circumstances. As a result, I found that the truth was God's Word. Simply said, He had not given me the spirit of fear but of power, of love, and of a sound mind. I can do all things through Christ who strengthens me. Don't try to do this with the power of positive thinking. Positive thinking is great, but it is not the sword of the spirit or the shield of faith. Positive faith in God can provide you the sword and shield and can make an absolute difference.

When I had only one jump left, everything seemed to be going wrong for me, and the negative thoughts kept pressing into my consciousness. I see now that these thoughts were fear trying to coax me to act on those thoughts. God says that with every temptation, He will provide the way of escape. After these thoughts went through my mind, God reminded me that I had committed to do the best I could for Him. He also reminded me of Philippians 4:13. This was my way of escape, but I had to put the scripture into action and act on the scripture. Hebrews 11:1 says, "Faith is the substance of things hoped for and the evidence of things not seen." James 2:17 says, "Faith without action is dead." Looking back, it is easy for me to see that I was going to win the nationals if I just acted on God's Word. I once heard a man say that fear is False Evidence Appearing Real. I'll buy that! God does not want us to be moved by what we see or hear but to be moved only by His Word. When I acted on God's Word, I found the truth.

As for God, His way is perfect; the word of the Lord is proven; He is a shield to all who trust in Him.

AFC

Psalm 18:30

Shields of Strength

CHAPTER FIFTEEN

SHIELDS OF STRENGTH

After winning the national championship, I found that what I had learned about fear also applies to my everyday life and to challenges far more important than winning a medal or a trophy. Good examples of this are the challenges of being a good husband and a good father. At times, I would fear letting Tammie or my family down so much that when I heard one of them complain about anything, I would overreact in anger to the fear and to them. Another big fear for me was failing on the job. Many times, that fear has actually hindered my job performance. In family and career challenges, I realize that fear sometimes moves me toward the very realities that I fear.

I wanted a daily reminder of God's Word but figured I would look silly carrying my water ski tow rope handles with me wherever I went. So I bought a few military-type dog tags and engraved the scriptures that I have mentioned on them. I wore them under my shirt as daily reminders for me. Each time I would be tempted with fear or anger or anything else that would hinder me, I would read my II Corinthians tag that says, "I cast down imaginations and every high thing that exalts itself against the knowledge of God and bring into captivity every thought to the obedience of Christ." Next I would read II Timothy 1:7: "For God has not given me the spirit of fear, but of power, of love, and of a sound mind." I found that what I had learned in winning the national championship could also help me win in life.

Over the next few months, people started noticing the dog tags that I wore, and I started getting requests for them. Soon, my little brother, Gabe, started calling the necklaces Shields of Strength. It is hard to believe what has come from the combination of my story and these simple Shields of Strength. I'll describe more of what has happened in the next section of this book, but let me say that millions of lives have been touched by God's grace through the simple idea of putting fear-breaking scriptures on some simple dog tags.

And there is another key, too. On the back of almost every Shield of Strength is inscribed the prayer we call the prayer of salvation. Prayers don't save anyone or get anyone to heaven, but a sincere decision to receive Jesus as your Lord and Savior will. Jesus said that anyone who comes to Him, He will not cast out. The Bible says that He stands at the door of our hearts, knocking, and He comes into the heart of anyone who will ask Him. The Shields of Strength are reminders of God's love, power, and faithfulness and an encouragement to act on His Word instead of fear. This is part of what has made the shields a global reminder of God's might for those in the midst of a righteous fight.

CHAPTER SIXTEEN

FROM TRIALS TO TROPHIES

I have always remembered that moment in 1996 at the national competition when I was standing alone by the lake after I was awarded my gold medal. Almost everyone had left, and I had time to myself to reflect and relive the events of the day. While thinking back on my last jump, I remembered taking off the remainder of the fin that broke when I hung my ski on the side of the ramp. And I remembered throwing it on the ground so I could quickly replace it with the new fin. I decided to walk back to the starting dock to see if I could find the broken fin. I saw it still lying where I had tossed it, so I picked it up and took it home with me as a souvenir of the day.

After a few months, I came to realize that I treasured that broken fin about as much as I treasured my gold medal. I consider that fin a trophy. If I had given up and not acted on God's Word, I would never have wanted to see that fin again. Today, I would give up my medal before I would part with that broken fin. For a while that seemed very strange to me. After all, that broken fin might have prevented me from accomplishing my dream. Even if I had not finished first, I still would have considered my broken fin a trophy because I acted on God's Word, doing the best I could for Him, and I did not quit until I was finished. Now that the trophy is mine, I am encouraged in everything I do, knowing that with Jesus I can do anything. I see how He moved me through the trials to receive the trophies. That broken fin is a symbol of this, and I will treasure it all my life.

Many times in life, people and things act against us to try to prevent us from accomplishing our dreams. The truth is God's Word that says, "We can do all things through Christ who strengthens us." The trials simply determine the depth of our character and the value of our testimony when we have done all things through Christ. God could have given me a national championship at the age of fourteen. After all, He is God. He can do anything. However, had I not faced all these trials, I would not be writing this book, I would not have made the first Shield of Strength, and I would not have anything to offer people. God is sometimes more interested in the process of our overcoming trials than He is in easily earned trophies.

Let me take this opportunity to tell you, straight out, to avoid the trials you can avoid without losing sight of your dreams. When you can't avoid a trial without losing sight of your dreams, roll up your sleeves, spend some time praying and reading God's Word, and then fight with power, love, and a sound mind until God delivers you. The cross was the greatest trial the world ever faced, yet today that cross is truly the world's greatest trophy. Thank God, Jesus followed through with his journey to the cross. Always remember—the greater the trial, the greater the trophy!

CHAPTER SEVENTEEN

SERVING OUR TROOPS

One of the great lessons of my life is that God does not just work in us for our own sake. He also works in us so that we can be trophies of His grace. He works in us so that we can become useful in taking His message to others. That God could do such a thing with my life humbles me to tears at the thought of it—that somehow He has used my experience to affect the American military at a time of great crisis in our nation and conflict both at home and abroad.

After everything occurred that you have read about in the first portion of this book—the battle with fear, the ministry of my wife, the victory over the enemies of my soul and the eventual championship—the Lord began to create opportunities for the shields to go everywhere. People would see me on the street and ask for them. We got e-mails requesting them, and some folks wanted them in large amounts. I was touched by this, but I could not have envisioned then all that was to come.

Late in 2001, I got a letter from the 86th Signal Battalion out of Fort Huachuca, Arizona. They were some of the first soldiers deployed to Afghanistan following the September 11 attacks on our country. They were shipping out in November, and they asked me if they could get five hundred shields for the men and women being deployed. Their commander was Lieutenant Colonel David Dodd; it turned out he was a man with a deep faith in God, and he wanted his soldiers to have something that would help them keep their spiritual focus. I can't tell you how moved I was. I had already been blown away that people had been asking for the shields. Now, the commander of an entire battalion of the American Army was asking for them. Of course I said yes. In fact, we not only sent them the five hundred they asked for; we also sent a hundred more so that Lieutenant Colonel Dodd would have some to give to other units.

Over the following months, I began hearing from the men and women who carried the shields into battle. They would talk about how they would recite the scriptures on the shields aloud before they went into battle or how they would grasp the shields while standing their post on a dark and nervous night. It was obvious that these little Shields of Strength, symbols of my own battle with paralyzing fear, were bringing encouragement and faith to our troops in the midst of their fierce battle.

Following a nine-month deployment in Afghanistan, the 86th Signal Battalion returned to Fort Huachuca to reset their equipment in preparation for their January 2003 deployment in support of Operation Iraqi Freedom. Tammie and I received an invitation to attend their battalion Christmas ball in Fort Huachuca. We were thrilled, of course. What an honor! We quickly agreed to go, and it turned out to be one of the great occasions of our lives. Lieutenant Colonel Dodd put us up in a general's quarters and took care of us with great kindness. At the ball, he seated us at the head table. Everyone kept coming up to us, telling us what the shields meant to him or her and thanking us for what we had done. What *we* had done? Man, here these soldiers had gone and fought for our freedom, and yet they were thanking us for what we had done. I was fighting back tears almost the whole night.

I was also fighting back a little bit of concern. You see, dog tags are something you are given when you become a solider. It is something you work for, something you earn. I had a concern that the soldiers would not be happy that I was wearing and making versions of their dog tags. I thought they might be offended that I was encouraging people to wear what they had not earned, what cost a soldier his blood, sweat, and tears. In other words, I was concerned that Lieutenant Colonel Dodd's soldiers wouldn't think much of me because I wasn't a soldier. When I mentioned this to him, he listened kindly with a slight smile on his face, already having a solution in mind. On the night of the ball, he surprised me by presenting me with the colors of the 86th Battalion, their flag, and he even made me an honorary soldier. As to the concern I had earlier expressed, he said, "Kenny, don't ever worry about that again."

Since then, Lieutenant Colonel Dodd and I have become lifelong friends, and I have learned from him and from his troops so much about the

American military. I have always had respect for our troops and for those who fight for us and defend our freedom. But as I got to know them better, I realized not only how amazing they are as warriors, but also that they are human beings with challenges, worries, and troubles. They have wives or husbands. They have children needing their attention. They have bills and in-laws and cars to maintain and hopes to fulfill in their lives. In other words, they are glorious heroes, but they are amazing, not in spite of the smaller challenges they face but because of them; they handle both the mundane things of life as well as the major military challenges of our time. I grew to love them and respect them more than ever.

Tammie and I were humbled and tearful after the honor we had been given. And then we had more reason to be humbled. Before we left, Lieutenant Colonel Dodd said that a commander at the Pentagon had called asking if Tammie and I would be willing to come and speak at a Pentagon breakfast. We did, and soon other military units began to contact us about the shields, and we began shipping orders to them. I remember one day I made up a flier for some Christian stores describing what units had requested the shields. There were eight units total, and I remember staring at that flier, amazed that we could serve so many soldiers. Naturally, I had no idea about what was to come.

One of the things that motivated me so much at the time was that I had this image in my mind. It was a picture of an old man taking down a box of his military gear years after he had left the military. In my imagination, he would rummage through that box and remember his days at war. And then he would come across the Shield of Strength that he had worn during his military days. He would remember how God had seen him through and how he had prayed, perhaps holding that shield in his hand. He would thank God for His grace and protection. Maybe the man would even commit himself to the Lord in a deeper way. I would think about a scene like this somewhere decades from now, and it would make me tear up. What a privilege to give our soldiers, airmen, Marines, and sailors something that would help build their faith.

One of the experiences I had that really confirmed the vision that was growing in my heart for the shields was a conversation I had with a soldier at that Christmas ball in Fort Huachuca. A young soldier told me what the shields had meant to him, and then he asked if I had ever written a book. He said he was eager to get all the lessons of my story in his heart and that he wanted to make sure he hadn't missed anything. His question got me thinking about how to affect people like him with my story, and so I sat down to write him a letter. That letter became the seed of this book, and I want to let you read it here. I'll include the letter I wrote Lieutenant Colonel Dodd asking that he help me find this young man.

December 23, 2002

Lieutenant Colonel David Dodd

U.S. Army

Fort Huachuca, AZ

Dear Lieutenant Colonel Dodd:

I am writing in hope that you can help me find a soldier in the 86th Signal Battalion. After I spoke at the Christmas ball, a soldier approached the head table to talk with me. He shook my hand and thanked me for sharing my testimony. He wanted to know if I had written a book about my story. He said he wanted to make sure he had not missed anything I said and would not forget any part of my message.

I told him I had not written a book, but if I ever did, I would give him a copy. After he walked away, I realized I did not know his name. This concerned me greatly because this soldier seemed to have a humble and sincere heart. I see those qualities as two of the most important qualities God uses to work in someone's life.

Since I had never written a book before, I wanted to write to this soldier in as much detail as possible some of what God has taught me about overcoming fear and living a life of victory.

This book is my letter to him. If you can find this soldier and deliver this letter, I would greatly appreciate it. He is the only soldier to ask me if I had written a book, so I hope he won't be hard to find.

Sincerely,
John Kennedy Vaughan

P.S. I remember hearing your talk to your men on Proverbs 27:17, "As iron sharpens iron, so one man sharpens another." Your words have helped me see the competition starting dock in a new light. Thank you for the insight your words on that principle have added to my life.

Dear Soldier of the 86th Battalion,
I hope Lieutenant Colonel Dodd finds you for me. I believe if anyone can find you, he can. I began writing a letter to you and ended up writing the book your question encouraged me to begin. I pray this message reaches you, and I pray that the truths and events I have recorded will provide encouragement to you and to others struggling to fight all kinds of battles, no matter how large or small.

Again, thank you for the sacrifices you and your family make for our country and for my family and me. All my life I was taught that anything worth having comes with a great price and I need to be willing to pay that price. However, two of the most important things in my life—my spiritual freedom and my physical freedom—have come at the greatest price, and I have not paid for either. Jesus paid for my spiritual freedom on the cross, and I thank Him for that every day. My physical freedom was and is still being paid for by the men and women of the United States military. Rarely do I get the chance to thank our military, but I want you to know I am extremely grateful.

You are one among the world's most highly trained soldiers—physically, technically, and academically. My prayer is that in high-pressure situations, you will be able to function with a sound mind and use all your training to the best of your ability, knowing God is with you.

I have learned that when everything is on the line, if I am not careful, fear can rob me of a sound mind and render all my training and preparation useless. All the training in the world will do you no good if you can't function with a sound mind. God does not want us to be moved by what we see or hear, only by His Word. I imagine a well-trained soldier fighting with fear is in great danger, but a well-trained soldier fighting with power, love, and a sound mind and acting on God's Word presents a great danger. God and His Word will help you overcome the fear that can rob you of a sound mind, slow your reflexes, dim your senses, cloud your judgment, and try to cancel out the skills you've acquired and all the physical training you have undergone. Thinking and acting on God's Word brings you great freedom, peace of mind, boldness, and an ability to act with a sound mind while using all your training and preparation to function to the best of your ability, no matter what the circumstances.

I wanted you to know that Command Sergeant Major Clay along with Colonel David Dodd saw the Shield of Strength necklaces in a Christian bookstore in Sierra Vista. Understanding the power of God's Word, Command Sergeant Major Clay wanted to get them to you guys before you deployed to the Middle East. That's when I got the letter requesting five hundred Shields of Strength for the 86th Signal Battalion. I over-nighted the tags and now hear that they were handed out as you guys boarded planes headed to Afghanistan.

On the back of most Shields of Strength is written a prayer called the prayer of salvation. Prayers don't save anyone or get anyone to heaven, but a sincere decision to receive Jesus as your Lord and Savior will. Jesus said that anyone who comes to Him, He will not cast out. He said He stands at the door of our hearts, knocking. For anyone who will answer that knock, He will come in to his or her heart. The Bible, in John 3:16 says, "For God so loved the world that He gave his only Son that whosoever believes in Him will not perish but have everlasting life." Romans 10:9–10 says, "For if you confess with your mouth that Jesus is Lord and believe in your heart that God raised Him from the dead, you will be saved. For it is by believing in your heart that you are made right with God, and it is by confessing with your mouth that you are saved." The prayer of salvation (on the back of the shields) is a simple prayer but a powerful and eternal decision. It reads "Dear Lord Jesus, I realize that I am a sinner. I repent for my sins and I receive you as my Lord and Savior." When a man or woman first makes this decision, he or she is then instantly filled with the power to overcome anything if he or she acts on God's Word. Best of all, that person has secured his or her place in eternity with Jesus.

The scripture on the first tags I sent to your battalion was from Joshua 1:9: "I will be strong and courageous. I will not be terrified or discouraged; for the Lord my God is with me wherever I go." Joshua was a great soldier who overcame great odds, fighting with power, love, and a sound mind while acting on God's Word.

Because members of the 86th Signal Battalion shared Shields of Strength with soldiers from other units, we have had calls every week from U.S. military chaplains requesting the necklaces. Shields of Strength are simply a reminder of God's Word. I pray they will serve to teach people the importance of having God's Word in their hearts. I also pray that the shields will help teach people to form the good habit of turning to God's Word, with or without a reminder, in times of trial and even when the waters are smooth.

When I give a tag away, I remember that my mind and heart can carry a lot more of God's Word than these tags can. Best of all, in times of trouble, God will bring to memory His words we have stowed in our hearts. I believe that the more of God's Word you have in your heart, the more you are prepared to face anything with a sound mind until finally there is nothing that will rock you. I have seen elderly men who cannot be moved with or without God's Word, and they are full of fear. And I have seen old men who are unshakeable because they depend on God's Word to keep them strong. Yet, these men are full of love, compassion, and wisdom. They are strong, but not hardened; bold, but not bitter; slow to anger, but quick to show gentleness and compassion. They are a source of God's wisdom and grace for many in times of trouble. You have a great opportunity to grow in God's Word. Your whole life will be blessed because you are challenged to endure all things with power, love, and a sound mind. Through your trials, God will build strong character within you.

I pray we will both become old men who cannot be shaken yet who are full of God's love and wisdom. When I see the United States armed forces, I see a gentle giant. Our country was built on Christ. The men who founded this country were Christians. We are by far the most powerful country in the world even though we are among the youngest. We cannot be moved, yet we are full of love and compassion.

I am thankful that God holds us in the shelter of His hand, and I am thankful He caused our paths to cross last year. I am glad you were bold enough to come talk with me and encourage me to write these words.

I guess God had this all planned. I don't consider myself to have any more favor in God's eyes than the next man or woman. Acts 10:34 tells us, "God is no respecter of persons." He loves you as much as me or anyone else. I am thankful He allowed me a trial too big to overcome on my own, a trial that forced me to trust Him completely through it. I am thankful God did not give up on me and that He sent me a girlfriend (who is now my wife) to bring me closer to the Truth that set me free. John 8:36 says, "He who the Son sets free is free indeed." I can testify to that!

I pray my story encourages you to find the same freedom and that in turn, your story encourages someone else to do the same. And if we never meet again on this earth, you can tell me your story as we walk together . . . along the streets of gold.

Sincerely, Your Brother in Christ,
John Kennedy Vaughan

"Be anxious for nothing, but in everything by prayer and supplication, with thanksgiving, let your requests be made

> known to God; and the peace of God,
> which surpasses all understanding,
> will guard your hearts and minds
> through Christ Jesus."
> —*Philippians 4:6–7*

The shields were becoming for the soldiers what my water-ski handle painted with scripture had become to me—a constant reminder of God's Word, and they symbolized the lessons I shared in my letter to the soldier. I think maybe that's what made them catch on and become so popular. Whatever it was, the demand for the shields soon skyrocketed. Before long, we got a request from the 82nd Airborne Division asking for five thousand shields. Five thousand! Up to now, we had made the shields with scriptures on them and with a sinner's prayer, but the 82nd asked that we also print their unit emblem. This was the first time we had gotten such a request, and it was exciting to think that such a heroic unit wanted our shields with their famous emblem on them.

Things took off from there. Over the next six months we went from getting a call for the shields maybe every two or three weeks to getting half a dozen calls a week. As 2003 unfolded, we were receiving two or three calls for shields a day. America had largely gained control on the ground in Afghanistan, and now President Bush was calling for the invasion of Iraq. We received many urgent calls for shields, including from a number of Ranger units, from the 4th Infantry Division, from the First Cavalry Division and from numerous others. I kept thinking as all this unfolded that all I ever intended was for the shields to be given to my fellow athletes and for them to be offered in a few Christian stores. God had other ideas. Now, I found that I was producing tens of thousands of shields, largely for our men and women in uniform. I was constantly humbled, constantly excited by what God was doing, and constantly amazed by how His purpose was bigger than my dream.

It was just about this time that a horrible tragedy occurred. In April of 2003, Captain Russell Rippetoe—son of Vietnam veteran Lieutenant Colonel Joe Rippetoe and his wife Rita—was killed in Iraq. Other officers had been killed in Afghanistan and would be killed in Iraq, but Rippetoe was exceptional not only because he died for his country but also because he was the first U.S. soldier killed in Iraq to be buried at Arlington National Cemetery. Because of this,

President Bush mentioned Captain Rippetoe in his Memorial Day speech that year, and the gear Rippetoe was wearing when he died was put on display at the Smithsonian. It turned out that he had died with a Shield of Strength around his neck—in fact, the President had read the scripture on Rippetoe's shield in his speech—and now, amazingly, one of our shields was on display in the Smithsonian Museum in our nation's capital. It was almost more than I could stand.

I was not really prepared for what was about to happen. After President Bush's speech, the Associated Press called me and wanted an interview. They said the story was intended only for regional release, but given its theme, it might go national. It did. Soon the whole nation was awakening to newspaper stories about the Shields of Strength that Captain Rippetoe and thousands of other soldiers carried. The *700 Club* called to do an interview as did *FOX News,* who sent a crew down to my home to tape segments for Brett Hume's show. There was more media and more attention, and soon we found ourselves at a whole new level.

Our Web site blew up. Within an hour of the first broadcast of some of my interviews, there were more than two thousand orders. The next day there were a thousand and then five hundred. It didn't really slow down after that. Soon, I realized that this was a major part of what God had called me to do. I took the income from the shields and used it to donate Shields of Strength to military chaplains and commanders who wanted Shields of Strength for their troops but did not have funds. I could not have known even then, though, that the day would come when I would celebrate with my family and staff the more than three million shields that would be sold or given away.

It has all been exciting and overwhelming, but I don't want to wrap up this story until I give you a chance to understand the wonder of what God is doing, the power of God's work with the shields. Perhaps the best way to do this is to let another man tell it.

In 2005, we started getting calls from people asking for Shields of Strength and saying they had read about them in a book called *The Faith of the American Soldier* by Stephen Mansfield. I knew Mansfield had written the mega-seller *The Faith of George W. Bush,* and I had seen him on TV a few times but did not know him personally. Blake Bradley, who handled most of our communication with the military, decided to visit our local bookstore and buy a copy of Mansfield's book to see what was said about Shields of Strength that had people calling. After reading part of the book, he came into my office and said, "The shields aren't just mentioned in passing. Mansfield tells the whole story of Rippetoe and how the shields are part of it." I got the book, read it, and couldn't believe it. I had never talked to Stephen Mansfield, but he had movingly captured Captain Rippetoe's story and described the shields in wonderful ways. I think it will help you understand what was going on then if I reprint that portion of Mansfield's book. Stephen Mansfield, who has become a friend now, gave me permission to include this.

CHAPTER EIGHTEEN

SHIELDS OF FAITH

It was April 3, 2003, and the United States had been in Iraq for almost two weeks. Captain Russell Rippetoe, along with Staff Sergeant Nino Livaudais, 23, and Specialist Ryan P. Long, 21, were inspecting cars with other soldiers of their company at a checkpoint some two hours outside of Baghdad. It was important work and they knew it. Near the checkpoint they guarded was a dam. If the insurgents were allowed to get close to that dam and blow it up, the villages nearby would be flooded. People would die, and the cause of liberty would suffer a serious blow. Captain Rippetoe understood this and so did his team. They went about their duties as though peace in the world depended upon it.

But then Russell Rippetoe had always lived life like a man on a mission. He was, after all, a member of the 75th Ranger Regiment, the unit whose heroism lives in modern memory through the film *Black Hawk Down.* Rippetoe wanted to live up to that reputation. It had bothered him, for example, that he hadn't had a chance to make a parachute jump into the Baghdad airport when his unit arrived in Iraq. The planned jump was abandoned, and Rippetoe and his team had made a normal runway landing. "I wanted to jump to see if I would hold up to the stress," he wrote in his journal, "and do my job to the standard of all the Rangers."

Rippetoe was always achieving, always striving to be the man of his inner vision. A soccer star, the homecoming king at his Colorado high school and an Eagle Scout, he had hoped to fly planes for the Air Force. His dyslexia killed that dream, though, and he decided instead to attend the University of Colorado, where he majored in management. After a few years he began eyeing the Army, and when he joined after graduation, he knew he had chosen well. First there was the training at Ft. Sill, followed by Artillery Basic. Along the way he got help for his dyslexia, and it was then that he began to spread his wings. He went to Ranger school and joined the famed 82nd Airborne at Ft. Bragg. When he landed in the 310 Field Artillery, he knew he'd found a home.

All this led to an assignment in Afghanistan. It seemed almost natural, somehow in the family tradition. Russell's father, Joe, had been a Ranger in Vietnam, and his uncles fought in World War II and Korea. An early American Rippetoe had even fought under George Washington. Afghanistan was simply the next stage in the family calling.

During his three months in country, Russell grew. He spent his down time playing soccer, wrestling with his buddies, and reveling in the ways of soldiers. And there was something else. He saw men die for the first time. It changed him. He pressed into his Christian roots, prayed often with his chaplain, and found a new passion for the Bible.

Somewhere along the way, someone gave him something that looked like his dog tag. It was called a Shield of Strength. On one side there was a picture of the American flag with the words "One Nation Under God," and on the other were the modified words of Joshua 1:9: "I will be strong and courageous. I will not be terrified, or discouraged; for the Lord my God is with me wherever I go." Russell carried the Shield of Strength with him and soon learned that thousands of his fellow soldiers did likewise. It was an inspiration to have confidence in God, a seal of martial unity through faith.

That faith went with him into Iraq. With his Shield of Strength around his neck and his ever-present Bible—the camouflage-covered one with "Ranger 3rd Battalion" printed on it—in his backpack, Captain Rippetoe led his men through the early days of the Iraqi conflict. This is how he came to be at that checkpoint, the one near the strategic dam, on April 3, 2003.

It was on that day that three white suburbans pulled up to the checkpoint. Rippetoe and his men eyed them carefully. Suddenly, an excited, screaming woman jumped from the back seat of one of the vehicles. "I'm hungry. I need food and water," she cried. Rippetoe, always concerned for the safety of his men, ordered everyone to "hold back" and began walking toward the woman to see how he could help. When the woman saw him drawing near, she hesitated. It must have been the signal. The driver of one of the white suburbans then detonated a bomb that blew a house-sized hole in the earth. Captain Russell Rippetoe and two of his men, Livaudais and Long, were killed. Others, wounded, survived to tell the tale of their captain's greatness.

Then began the grieving—and the haunting sense of destiny. When Captain Rippetoe's father went to Ft. Benning, Georgia, to collect his son's belongings, there was a note from the young officer attached to his wall locker. The simple, prophetic words betrayed the truth that Russell had known even before leaving for Iraq that he would never go home again. "I want a military funeral," he had written, "and I want it to be my people."

And so it was. On the 10th of April, 2003, Captain Russell Rippetoe became the first American from the war in Iraq to be buried at Arlington National Cemetery. He was attended in death by his family and his fellow Rangers—the ones he had called "his people." And there were medals. The Army Rangers presented Captain Rippetoe's stricken parents with his two Bronze Stars for valor and a Purple Heart. There was also the American flag, the one from their son's coffin.

A few months later, President Bush honored Captain Rippetoe in his May 26 Memorial

Day speech. After quoting the words of Joshua 1:9 from the slain man's Shield of Strength, the president then said, "This faithful Army captain has joined a noble company of service and sacrifice gathered row by row. These men and women were strong and courageous and not dismayed. And we pray they have found their peace in the arms of God."

It is a story that seems destined to live on. At the Smithsonian Museum in Washington, D.C., there is an exhibit that includes the personal effects of Captain Rippetoe. Visitors to the museum can see the Ranger's gear—his helmet, goggles, web gear, boots, and uniform. These are no surprise. But then there are the symbols of the heart. Also on display is Rippetoe's Bible—the one with Ranger 3rd Battalion on it and the Ranger slogan: "Rangers Lead the Way." There is also a small cross, a second Bible, the Captain's dog tags and small piece of metal that was scorched in the explosion that took the man's life. It is the Shield of Strength, the words of Joshua 1:9 still clear.

Now, in the evening of his life, Russell Rippetoe's father often returns to Arlington to visit his son's grave—Number 7860, Section 60. When he does, he never finishes his vigil without leaving one of the Shields of Strength atop his son's stone marker. It is an act that honors his son and reminds other visitors of the passion that gave his son's life meaning. The young man's father knows that now hundreds of thousands of the little shields have gone out into the world and that Rangers the world over carry them to honor their God and their fallen comrades.

They carry the little shields, too, so that faith will rise in their own hearts. The words they carry are taken from the words of God to Joshua when he was just about to enter the promised land of his day. Now, centuries later, soldiers strive to enter the promised land of their own destiny and of their national purpose. As they do, they are often reciting—in the barrens of Afghanistan, the rocky crags of Iraq—the meditation of an ancient warrior: "I will be strong and courageous. I will not be terrified, or discouraged; for the Lord my God is with me wherever I go."

Captain Russell Rippetoe's story is a moving tale, a blend of themes that have emerged from battlefields for generations and the style of a new generation at war. The ancient in his tale is easy to see. He was an idealistic young officer who wanted to serve his country's cause but test his own mettle along the way. When confronted with hardship and death, he drank from the wells of faith his early religious training had dug for him. He prayed, studied, and celebrated his faith with others in the few moments of devotion that war allowed him. Then, while attempting to serve a people not his own, he died and was grieved by his family, lauded by his president, and given an honored place to rest in the capital of his country.

Most of these themes are as old as Homer and common to every war. Yet there is much that speaks of the new in Rippetoe's story. The passionate informality of the faith he found in the field is typical of his younger tribe at war. Moreover, this faith was inspired, in part, by a tiny Shield of Strength then popular among his fellow Rangers. It is almost the classic Millennial military icon: fashioned by a professional athlete who preaches "Xtreme Faith," sold on a web site—www.shieldsofstrength.com—and made, upon Rippetoe's death, a symbol of valor for a new generation that has now reached millions. There is one in the Oval Office, many in the pockets of Congressmen and Senators, and it is the emblem most often carried by members of the military in Afghanistan and Iraq aside from the official insignias they wear.

The popularity of the Shields of Strength may well be part of an attempt by Millennials to apply their faith, however informal it may be, to the demands of armed conflict. Every faith fashions some kind of code when it marches off to war. Millennial faith will be no different. It, too, will evolve a set of martial values, a corresponding code of ethics, slogans, and symbols. It, too, will guide the fighting of the young.

I was touched by Mansfield's description. It humbled me to think that God has so used the shields that a book on the faith of America's warriors would include anything that had to do with me. But then Mansfield went even further. After his book on soldiers was such a huge success, he decided to write a little gift book in which he told some "hero tales" that he had not had a chance to tell in the first book. This time, Stephen and I spoke before he wrote it, and he even invited me to have a page promoting the shields in the back of the book. One of the stories in the book was about my battle with fear and the story of the shields. I want to include it here— even though, in my opinion, I did not belong in this book along with such real American heroes—

because I want you to understand how God was using the shields those years ago and how He continues to use them now. This is a piece from Mansfield's book *American Heroes*.

CHAPTER NINETEEN

DIGGING A WELL OF INSPIRATION

He is not a soldier. He is a long distance water-ski jumper. He is not stationed in Afghanistan or Iraq. He lives in Beaumont, Texas. Yet his battle to conquer an enemy of his soul has meant inspiration for thousands on America's battlefields, and so it is that his story is linked now with the story of the American soldier.

Kenny Vaughan had the potential to be among the top long distance water-ski jumpers in the country. He was good, very good, and he wanted be the best. So, like all athletes who dream of championships,

Kenny worked hard, refusing to be satisfied with his last performance.

He knew his conditioning and his skills were ready for the ultimate challenge, but there was something working against his soul that threatened to bring defeat. It was fear. Though he had known many successes, fear of failure crippled Kenny. He heard its haunting voice as he suited up for a competition or as he sped toward the ramp before a jump. It distracted him, taunted him, and drained him of the courage and concentration he needed to do his best.

He had almost decided that he would never conquer this fear when he read Matthew 21:22: "If you believe, you will receive whatever you ask for in prayer." Kenny realized that if he truly trusted his God, he should ask for freedom from the fear that was robbing him and then trust that the answer would come. Kenny understood that his job was simply to have faith. And it worked. The fear that had robbed him of so much in his life began leaving his soul.

Some months later, Kenny went to the USA Water-Ski National Championships. Though he tore a ski boot in his second attempt, his third attempt was good enough to win him the championship. Kenny Vaughan fulfilled his dream of being the best long distance water-ski jumper in the nation.

Asked about it afterward, Kenny said that one of the reasons he jumped so far was that on that third attempt, when fear might have gripped him, he looked down and saw that his wife had written a scripture on his tow rope. It made all the difference, and he rode that wave of faith to victory.

Kenny had learned the power of words, particularly the words of the Bible, to inspire the human heart in the heat of battle. He decided in time to begin putting words of inspiration on dog tags so that others who strove to be champions could wear them and be strengthened in their faith. Kenny's brother thought of a name for the little dog tags: Shields of Strength, based on the Bible verse that describes God as a shield and a strength to the faithful.

Kenny could not have been prepared for what happened next. The Shields of Strength became wildly popular. He could hardly keep up with the demand. What moved him most, though, was the demand for the Shields of Strength among soldiers overseas. Tens of thousands of the little dog tags are now in Afghanistan and Iraq. Soldiers carry them in their pockets or around their necks. They recite the verses on them and even kiss them before battle as a touchstone of faith.

They are more than trinkets of belief, though. When Captain Russell Rippetoe, whose story is told in this book, was horribly killed in Iraq, he was carrying a Shield of Strength in his pocket. When the Smithsonian Museum put Rippetoe's gear on display, the Shield of Strength—burned at the edges from the explosion that killed the Captain—solemnly testified to the young officer's faith.

Likewise, Lt. Daniel Morales carried a Shield of Strength. When he wrote his university professor and challenged him to rethink the meaning of America's cause in the war, he put a Shield of Strength in the envelope. It was one of the best ways he knew to show the professor what he believed.

There are thousands of soldiers like Rippetoe and Morales who draw inspiration for combat from a little piece of metal that reminds them of their faith and a God Who is near. All of this began, though, when Kenny Vaughan decided not to let fear control his life. Now, he has dug a well of faith and inspiration for American soldiers around the world.

It was so hard for me to believe that somehow my battle with fear and the resulting Shields of Strength were now featured in two books. Sometimes I still can't believe it. Still, I knew it wasn't really about me. It was about the power of God's Word and how He allowed me to play a role in helping to share it with others. Needless to say, once Mansfield's books hit the bookstands, more doors began to open. And it has continued to be this way ever since. We have produced millions of shields. AAFES—Army and Air Force Exchange Service—are now carrying the shields in their stores on military bases all over the world. And I, a kid from Beaumont, Texas, have had the privilege of speaking at the Pentagon, Armed

Forces Command, and at gatherings of soldiers around the country.

I'm still amazed at what has come from my battle with fear and from the Lord teaching me how to overcome it. But if I could have chosen any place for what God has done in me to be of impact, I would have chosen the American military. I love those people. I respect them. I need them. And I will always work to serve them as I can. Clearly, the Lord feels almost exactly the same way! Look at what he has done through our simple story and through a simple idea like the shields.

EPILOGUE

Now, a few years later, I am still trying to win my second National Championship. I won the bronze at the nationals in 2003. That day I was skiing with so much boldness and confidence, I went for a huge jump and the win. I hit a perfect jump and did exactly what I wanted to do, but I forgot to make sure I kept the sound mind part going when I underestimated and failed to adjust for a strong tail wind. That was my only crash all year, but the force of the fall broke a bone in my foot, a Lisfranc injury, that was difficult to heal and required surgery. Everything would have been great if there had not been that strong tail wind. Another lesson learned. Never stop asking God for wisdom. As soon as you get too confident, you go out on your own and hit a brick wall.

I was recovering well but got off to a late start for the 2004 season. However, I didn't plan on letting that stop me from winning. I'd been skiing better than ever against much younger skiers who were raising the bar. The most amazing part is that I have skied with that same boldness the Lord gave me at the Nationals in 1996 for every tournament since, no matter how tough the competition or what I've had thrown at me. I was looking forward to Nationals 2004. The competition was in West Palm Beach, where the whole fear thing started. I couldn't wait to go back and ski that site with the boldness Christ had given me. However, two days before I would fly out for the nationals, another trial presented itself. During one of my last practices of the season, I crashed while landing a jump and broke my right arm.

The following year, 2005 was off to a great start before I somehow allowed the rope to get under my ski while I was about a hundred feet off the jump flying through the air. The result was that I dislocated my left knee completely tearing my ACL, MCL, and PCL with a partial tear of my only other ligament, my LCL. Doctors originally told me I would walk again but might not run or ski. I was referred to a Houston, Texas, doctor and wife team by the name of Dr. Walter and Dawn Lowe. Dr. Lowe is the lead physician for the Houston Texans, Rockets, and the chief physician for the University of Texas medical clinic. In my first visit with Dr. Lowe, he told me I had sustained a bad injury but he believed he could repair the damage.

My surgery was successful, and with the help of Dan Kroesch, my personal trainer and good friend, I have regained my strength and recovered completely. I will be back on the water this spring but not by myself this time. My training time will now be shared with Faith Vaughan, my nine-year-old daughter (who is skiing better than her daddy was at her age) and Grace Vaughan, my six-year-old who is already skiing and loves to ride the disk her grandfather (my dad) cut out of a sheet of plywood and painted the same color as the first one I rode. Tammie is even starting to get out from behind the camera and ski with us. It is a little more difficult for her though since our son, John Kennedy Vaughan, Jr., just turned one year old.

You know, I really thought after winning the Nationals in 1996 I would win dozens more. I just felt so complete, having found my way to the top of my game both physically and spiritually. I had no idea that now some fourteen years later I would not have won another one and, worst of all, that I would have suffered more and worse injuries than I ever had before. You know, I have watched many of my competitors ski now for twenty plus years and never suffer a serious injury. I don't know why my road went the way it did. But you know, when I think about it, I would have never made the first Shield of Strength if I had not suffered more than most. It is true there are no guarantees in life and you can give everything you have only to see all the wheels fall off, time and again. I just hope that I always get up one more time than I give up. My prayer is that my children will see, through my life, an example of true faith and confidence in a Heavenly Father who is always there; who disciplines and guides with love, grace, and mercy; and who knows the plan He has for each one of us.

I am blessed with what God has shown me and how He is using my struggles to bring others closer to Him. I am thankful for each day and for the way He has taught me to view the tests that life presents to me. I still look at that gold medal every night before I go to bed and think of all it represents in my life and in the life of so many others now. I have learned that you really have no idea what God has in store for you and that if He has not placed you there yet, it may be because you are not ready. Maybe what you are going through now is getting you ready for something bigger than you ever dreamed. Get up one more time. Don't quit now. You can do it. You really can do all things through Christ who strengthens you, and when you do, that one moment will change you and everyone you touch forever. In your own battle, it only takes one good blow to turn the tide in your favor and change the world as you know it. It takes only one!

ABOUT THE AUTHOR

(This overview of Kenny Vaughan's life was compiled by freelance writer Marcia Davis from interviews with Kenny Vaughan, his friends, and his family.)

John Kennedy Vaughan's father named him after the late John F. Kennedy, Jr.—from the image of that little boy saluting his slain father's flag-covered coffin as the funeral procession made its way toward Arlington National Cemetery. The small boy's relentless courage and honor in the face of overwhelming adversity was something John Kennedy Vaughan's father wanted to pass on to his son. And many say that, indeed, John Kennedy (Kenny) Vaughan's life has been marked with that very same courage and honor.

Kenny Vaughan lives his life driven by a stubborn faith, a quest for excellence that he pursues with uncompromising determination, a gentle spirit that is sensitive to others, and a heart wide open to God. Vaughan steps up to personal and professional challenges with confidence based on careful reasoning, considerable prayer, and mighty faith in a powerful God. In short, his life mirrors his faith and fortitude.

After he learned to ski at age eleven, his heart was set on becoming a champion water-skier. When he met and married his wife Tammie, he also set his heart toward being the best husband he could be. After their children Faith, Grace, and Kennedy were born, his purpose broadened to include being the best dad to them he could be. Later, when he started his own business, this same quest for excellence permeated his entrepreneurial pursuits.

As a champion athlete commissioned to share his faith, Kenny Vaughan's mission has stretched from the organization he founded in 1998—Athletes for Christ—to the four corners of the globe. He made his first Shields of Strength scripture-inscribed dog tags in 1997, never realizing the impact they would have in the years to come or the number of people who would be comforted and encouraged by wearing them.

His first dog tags were personal keepsakes to help him remember all that God had shown him about living in faith and overcoming fear while he competed in the U.S. Nationals ski jump competition. As friends, associates, and even total strangers saw the dog tags and asked Vaughan about them, he would take them off and give them away. Soon, he found himself giving away so many and receiving so many other requests for them from remote places that it became more economical to mass produce the dog tags instead of ordering individual replacements for himself.

When U.S. troops were first deployed to Afghanistan, shortly after the terrorist attacks of September 11, 2001, Command Sergeant Major Jacqui Clay requested Shields of Strength for the troops in her charge. It wasn't long before U.S. soldiers of every rank and in every military branch began wearing the necklaces alongside their military-issued dog tags. Military families at home began wearing the shields as a form of spiritual connection to their family members in military service or in memory or honor of lost loved ones who had made the ultimate sacrifice in the fight for freedom in Afghanistan and Iraq.

In December 2003, Vaughan was invited by his good friend Lieutenant Colonel David Dodd to share his story at a Pentagon prayer breakfast for military officers. After his talk, Kenny was able to personally greet each officer and hand each one a Shield of Strength. At the Pentagon, he met several high-ranking government officials who wore the Shields of Strength and who said their family members wore them as well. He was greeted by Acting Secretary of the Army and also by retired Colonel Les Brownlee. Dodd presented him with a flag encased with an inscription proclaiming "This flag was flown in Baghdad, Iraq, in honor of Mr. Kenny Vaughan. America's soldiers salute you for sharing God's Word and for providing Shields of Strength to empower them during Operation Enduring Freedom and Operation Iraqi Freedom."

During his Washington trip, Kenny was joined by retired Lieutenant Colonel Joe Rippetoe, the father of Capt. Russell B. Rippetoe, the first American soldier of Operation Iraqi Freedom to be buried in Arlington National Cemetery. When Captain Rippetoe was killed, he was wearing his Shield of Strength dog tag alongside his military-issued tag. Both Dodd and Rippetoe accompanied Vaughan to the Pentagon breakfast and later to visit Arlington Memorial Cemetery, where a burial service was underway, honoring another fallen soldier. That day Vaughan and Dodd looked in on several injured soldiers at Walter Reed Hospital. Of that trip, Vaughan later said, "In a year I usually realize a few defining moments, but this one day, which I will never forget, was an epiphany—truly one of the most memorable times I have known."

By 2010, Vaughan had made over three million Shields of Strength. By then, the dog tags were being worn by hundreds of thousands of U.S. military men and women serving in the Middle East and across the globe and by journalists covering the war in Iraq. Today, war veterans, athletes, youth, and adults in all walks of life find confidence and comfort in wearing the shields and encouragement in the scriptures inscribed on them.

Kenny Vaughan has been described as humble to a fault. He leads without show, giving his best and striving to achieve with an intense purpose, with neither pride nor pretense. Kenny seems to bring forth the best in others. He's quick to say his successes reflect God's glory.

Those who've met Kenny notice the steady gaze of sea-blue eyes, the quick flash of his friendly smile, a firm handshake, and a kind and caring countenance that puts one instantly at ease. The disciplined training of an elite athlete is evident in his build and carriage, and a Texas accent graces his soft-spoken manner. He is polite, sincere, engaging, and encouraging. It's obvious that Kenny Vaughan has an unquenchable desire to be used by God.

Kenny lives with his wife and three children in Beaumont, Texas, where he continues to compete as a USA National water ski jump champion. He also continues to be sought out by national print and broadcast media for interviews, and he continues to share his story at athletic, military, and Christian gatherings across the country.

How you can get your own Shield of Strength

Visit **www.shieldsofstrength.com** to see the wide assortment of Shields of Strength available. Once there, you'll find a pleasing array of military, occupational, and sports related Shields, as well as the immensely popular original designs. In addition, you'll find a section of recommended books, Shield accessories, and other beautiful jewelry pieces.

While you're there, be sure to check out our section devoted to testimonials. You'll be inspired by the many heartwarming stories shared by those who have either given or received a Shield of Strength. We promise you'll be touched.

Please consider giving to the
Shields of Strength Foundation.

Help us reach the world with the power of God's Word through your charitable donations to the Shields of Strength Foundation. This non-profit 501(c)(3) corporation's sole mission is to give away as many Shields of Strength as possible. Over the years, we've given hundreds of thousands of Shields to various ministries, charities, and military personnel. It's our sincerest hope that, with help from generous donors like you, we'll be able to give away many more thousands, or even millions, in the years to come.

Please visit our Web site at
www.shieldsofstrength.com and click
on the Shields of Strength Foundation
link for more information.

Shields of Strength Foundation 501(c)(3)
1555 S. Major Dr. | Beaumont, TX 77707
1.800.326.7882 | www.shieldsofstrength.com

ENJOY THIS BOOK BY
Chuck Holton

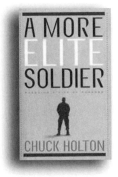

For other books by Chuck Holton, please visit **www.livefire.us.** The rigor of becoming an Airborne Ranger is exceeded only by the challenge of being one—but those who join their ranks find fulfillment in something bigger than themselves. In the same way, pursuing God's objectives energizes our everyday lives. Former U.S. Army Ranger Chuck Holton shows how God oversees our training and gives each of us specific skills to help us accomplish the mission He has for us in this great spiritual war. Riveting action and powerful vignettes offer potent spiritual ammunition for the battles of every Christian serving in God's army. Find out what it takes to be a more elite soldier.